DATE DUE

VENUS and SERENA WILLIAMS

**Recent Titles in
Greenwood Biographies**

Jack Kerouac: A Biography
Michael J. Dittman

Mother Teresa: A Biography
Meg Greene

Jane Addams: A Biography
Robin K. Berson

Rachel Carson: A Biography
Arlene R. Quaratiello

Desmond Tutu: A Biography
Steven D. Gish

Marie Curie: A Biography
Marilyn Bailey Ogilvie

Ralph Nader: A Biography
Patricia Cronin Marcello

Carl Sagan: A Biography
Ray Spangenburg and Kit Moser

Sylvia Plath: A Biography
Connie Ann Kirk

Jesse Jackson: A Biography
Roger Bruns

Franklin D. Roosevelt: A Biography
Jeffery W. Coker

Albert Einstein: A Biography
Alice Calaprice and Trevor Lipscombe

Stephen Hawking: A Biography
Kristine Larsen

Bill Russell: A Biography
Murry R. Nelson

VENUS and SERENA WILLIAMS

A Biography

Jacqueline Edmondson

GREENWOOD BIOGRAPHIES

GREENWOOD PRESS
WESTPORT, CONNECTICUT · LONDON

Library of Congress Cataloging-in-Publication Data

Edmondson, Jacqueline.
   Venus and Serena Williams : a biography / Jacqueline Edmondson.
      p. cm. — (Greenwood biographies, ISSN 1540–4900)
   Includes bibliographic references and index.
   ISBN: 0–313–33165–0 (alk. paper)
   1. Williams, Venus, 1980– 2. Williams, Serena, 1981– 3. Tennis players—United
States—Biography. 4. African American women tennis players—Biography. I. Title.
II. Series.
GV994.A1E36   2005
796.342'092'2—dc22   2005012720

British Library Cataloguing-in-Publication Data is available.

Library of Congress Catalog Card Number: 2005012720
ISBN: 0–313–33165–0
ISSN: 1540–4900

First published in 2005

Greenwood Press, 88 Post Road West, Westport, CT 06881
An imprint of Greenwood Publishing Group, Inc.
www.greenwood.com

Printed in the United States of America

The paper used in this book complies with the
Permanent Paper Standard issued by the National
Information Standards Organization (Z39.48–1984).

10 9 8 7 6 5 4 3 2 1

For my sons, Jacob and Luke
And for my nieces, Anna, Lindsay, and Megan

CONTENTS

Series Foreword   ix

Acknowledgments   xi

Introduction   xiii

Timeline for Venus Williams   xvii

Timeline for Serena Williams   xix

Chapter 1   Knowing the Possibilities in Life   1

Chapter 2   The Williams Family   9

Chapter 3   Venus   21

Chapter 4   Serena   31

Chapter 5   Tennis   43

Chapter 6   Controversies and Challenges in Tennis   63

Chapter 7   Celebrity, Fashion, and Beyond   77

Chapter 8   How Big a Deal It Is   87

Appendixes:

            Appendix A: Grand Slam Events   93

            Appendix B: Glossary of Terms   94

Appendix C: Venus Williams's Records and Awards   96

Appendix D: Serena Williams's Records and Awards   98

Appendix E: A Note on Sources   103

References   105

Index   111

Photo essay follows page 42

SERIES FOREWORD

In response to high school and public library needs, Greenwood developed this distinguished series of full-length biographies specifically for student use. Prepared by field experts and professionals, these engaging biographies are tailored for high school students who need challenging yet accessible biographies. Ideal for secondary school assignments, the length, format and subject areas are designed to meet educators' requirements and students' interests.

Greenwood offers an extensive selection of biographies spanning all curriculum related subject areas including social studies, the sciences, literature and the arts, history and politics, as well as popular culture, covering public figures and famous personalities from all time periods and backgrounds, both historic and contemporary, who have made an impact on American and/or world culture. Greenwood biographies were chosen based on comprehensive feedback from librarians and educators. Consideration was given to both curriculum relevance and inherent interest. The result is an intriguing mix of the well known and the unexpected, the saints and sinners from long-ago history and contemporary pop culture. Readers will find a wide array of subject choices from fascinating crime figures like Al Capone to inspiring pioneers like Margaret Mead, from the greatest minds of our time like Stephen Hawking to the most amazing success stories of our day like J.K. Rowling.

While the emphasis is on fact, not glorification, the books are meant to be fun to read. Each volume provides in-depth information about the subject's life from birth through childhood, the teen years, and adulthood.

A thorough account relates family background and education, traces personal and professional influences, and explores struggles, accomplishments, and contributions. A timeline highlights the most significant life events against a historical perspective. Bibliographies supplement the reference value of each volume.

ACKNOWLEDGMENTS

Thanks to Paul Vinhage, Kurt Vinhage, Frank Gallagher, and Nick Gallagher for their wonderful advice on the content and form of this book.

Thanks to Dr. Murry Nelson for his encouragement and influence on this project, for much conversation about the content and form of this book, and for providing key resources for me as the research for this project took shape.

Thanks to Christopher Robbins for conversations on race in American society and for providing key resources that helped me to think through issues of race and culture in contemporary contexts.

Special thanks to Luke and Jacob for noticing newspaper articles, magazine articles, and television coverage of Venus and Serena and for commenting on the book as it was being written. Special thanks to Michael for countless conversations about this project and for reading through it so many times.

INTRODUCTION

Venus and Serena Williams charged onto center court in professional tennis at the end of the twentieth century with a force never before seen in the sport. No other women tennis players had matched their strength, their speed, or their overall athleticism, and none had achieved the status and celebrity they gained on and off the court as they powered to the number one and two rankings in the Women's Tennis Association (WTA). Their entrance onto the stage of major tournaments around the world was not a quiet one, and while they tried to preserve some measure of privacy, at least initially, their lives off the court became just as colorful and decorated as their fame grew.

Studying Venus and Serena Williams is important for anyone interested in learning more about American culture and the history of sport at the turn of the twenty-first century. We often think of pioneers as people who have gone where no one else had gone before. This certainly applies to Venus and Serena. They represent in many ways a shift in attitudes concerning women in sports, particularly African American women. As they played tough tennis, they conveyed to the public that it was acceptable for women to be strong, to have muscles, and to compete. Venus and Serena marched onto the court and into the public eye with their hair bound in beads that spoke of their ethnic pride, with braces on their teeth that belied their youth, and with much grit to withstand challenges concerning the attitudes of these young black women in what had traditionally been a white-washed sport. There is no doubt they will have a lasting impact on tennis, sports history, and American culture. This book shares their stories, and it provides a way to consider the impact of race, gender, and culture and the influence these have through sport in shaping popular culture.

Biographies are important tools in understanding trends and movements in societies. They allow us to connect our lives with those of others so that we might better understand culture, history, and possibilities for the future. As writer Mary Catherine Bateson has observed, reading biographies gives us perspectives on our lives. They help us to compare, to understand choices and circumstances that people faced in order to come to terms with society at large, and to consider some of the options we face as well. They serve to inspire and to teach. Yet Bateson also warned that biographies risk telling stories of the lives of people as though there is some well-delineated quest, some journey through time toward an end that is specific, predetermined, and concrete. Such an idealist retelling of a person's life is not particularly realistic, nor is it necessarily helpful for readers. Instead, Bateson suggested that it is best to tell human stories as they are: continually in the process of being redefined amid circumstances and conditions that may or may not have been anticipated. She encouraged the study of the "creative potential of interrupted and conflicted lives, where energies are not narrowly focused or permanently pointed toward a single ambition" (Bateson, 1989, p. 9).

It seems that Venus and Serena Williams's story allows such a telling. No one would have predicted the immense success these sisters achieved, seemingly against all odds, as they worked their way from the ghetto to keep company with some of the top-paid women athletes. And now, it is difficult to predict what direction they may take in the future. Many speculate about how long their careers in tennis will continue, and they seem to have many possibilities ahead of them both on and off the tennis court. Their lives are taking directions that they determine, yet these directions are influenced by society at large, by histories that have preceded them, and by possibilities they imagine for the future.

Although they are yet quite young (Venus is 24 at the time of this writing, and Serena is 23), Venus and Serena's stories are replete with challenge, controversy, and struggle. Yet they have persevered, achieving by the time they were young adults much more than anyone could have anticipated. Theirs is not a story simply told of two kids rising up from the ghetto to become great tennis players, although this is a powerful story in and of itself. Instead, Venus and Serena's story is even more complex. This is a story of two sisters who were members of a family that faced joys and sorrows together, like any family would, amid oppressive and racially hostile social and economic conditions. This is a story of two daughters who tried to hold true to their father's charge that tennis was not enough; instead, they needed a good education and other interests in order to be considered successful. This is a story of two African American women who refused to be defined by others; instead they took charge and carved their own identities that honored their ghetto past, their religion, and their family as they strove toward a different future for themselves. In so doing, they paved the way for many young people—African American, poor urban kids, and others—to imagine different possibilities for themselves.

The purpose of this biography is not to idealize Venus and Serena as heroes or to make them appear superhuman. While their stories are inspirational, this book includes discussion of controversies and challenges in their lives because we can learn from these as well. Any person's life has contradictions, flaws, and errors, and to the extent possible, these are told here.

The circumstances and accomplishments of Venus and Serena's lives give us pause as we consider the circumstances and accomplishments of our own lives and the ways in which these intersect with each other and society at large. Their story will inspire, and it will help us as we work toward a more just and equitable society as we face difficult questions of race, gender, and social class amid broader decisions of how we wish to live together.

TIMELINE FOR
VENUS WILLIAMS

1980   Born Venus Ebony Starr Williams in Longwood, California, on June 20.

1984   Made first trips to a tennis court in Compton, California, with father, Richard.

1989   Visited Chris Evert's home to admire trophies.

1990   Served ball at 100 miles per hour. Featured in *New York Times* article.

1991   Williams family moved to Florida. Enrolled in Rick Macci's tennis academy. Although Venus held 63–0 record on USTA junior tour and was ranked first in the 12 and under division, Richard pulled her off the junior circuit.

1994   Turned professional on October 31, 1994. Won her first professional match against Shaun Stafford at Bank of the West Classic in California.

1995   Conducted a clinic with Serena and Richard for the California Tennis Association. This grew into the Venus and Serena Williams Tutorial Tennis Academy. Signed a $12 million contract with Reebok. Withdrew from Macci's tennis academy.

1997   Graduated from high school at the Driftwood Academy in Lake Park, Florida. She went on to complete classes at the Art Institute in Florida and to earn a certificate in interior design from Palm Beach Community College.

TIMELINE FOR VENUS WILLIAMS

1998   Launched *Tennis Monthly Recap* with Serena. Won first doubles event with Serena. Won mixed doubles with American Justin Gimblestob at Australian Open.

1999   Faced Serena in the Lipton Championships on March 28. Appeared on 10 episodes of *Hollywood Squares* with Serena.

2000   Purchased a $2.7 million mansion in Palm Beach, Florida, with Serena.
        Won Wimbledon (first Grand Slam singles victory) and U.S. Open. Signed a $40 million contract with Reebok. Won singles gold at Olympic Games in Sydney, Australia. Won doubles gold with Serena. Kerrie Brooks became her trainer. With Serena, defeated Navratilova and DeSwardt in doubles final at Wimbledon.

2001   Won Wimbledon and U.S. Open. Faced Serena in U.S. Open finals during prime time. Made guest appearance with Serena on *The Simpsons*. Doll made in her image.

2002   Founded *Vstarr Interiors* in April. Appeared on *Oprah Winfrey Show* in November. Held No. 1 ranking on the WTA.

2003   Sister Yetunde Price murdered in September.

2004   Coauthored tennis book with Serena. Played in Olympic Games in Athens, Greece.

TIMELINE FOR
SERENA WILLIAMS

1981   Born in Saginaw, Michigan, on September 26.

1985   Began to play tennis in Compton, California, with Venus and father, Richard.

1991   Moved with family to Florida. Had 46–3 record on junior USTA tour. Ranked first in the 10 and under division.

1995   Turned professional in September. Conducted clinic with Venus and Richard for the California Tennis Association. This later grew into the Venus and Serena Williams Tutorial Tennis Academy.

1997   Began the season ranked 304. Ended season ranked 99.

1998   Graduated high school. Signed $12 million deal with Puma. Won mixed doubles with Max Mirnyi of Belarus at U.S. Open and Wimbledon.

1999   Faced sister Venus in finals at Lipton Championships in Key Biscayne, Florida. Won U.S. Open (first Grand Slam for Serena and the Williams family).

2000   Purchased $2.7 million mansion with Venus in Palm Beach, Florida. Won gold medal in Olympic women's double final with Venus.

2001   Indian Wells tournament controversy (March). Ranked No. 1 by WTA (held ranking for 57 weeks). Guest appearance with Venus on *The Simpsons*. Cameo appearance in movie *Black Knight*. Doll made in her image.

2002   Won French Open, Wimbledon, and U.S. Open. Purchased $1.4 million condominium in West Side, California. Stalked by German Albrecht Stromeyer. Appeared as school teacher on *My Wife and Kids* and with her sisters and mother on *Oprah Winfrey Show*.

2003   Won the Australian Open to complete Serena Slam. Won Wimbledon. Appeared on *Street Time* and filmed a short part in *Beauty Shop*. In July, sister Yetunde accompanied Serena to 11th annual ESPY awards. Launched *Aneres*. In September, sister Yetunde was murdered.

Chapter 1

KNOWING THE POSSIBILITIES IN LIFE

They weren't allowed to say C-A-N-'-T. I didn't allow that because I didn't want them to set limitations for themselves. I hope that black youth see in them strength, power, and growth, and knowing all the possibilities in life. Whatever it is that their goal is in life, that they can do it and they can achieve it and be strong at it and be good at it.

Oracene Price on Venus and Serena Williams,
The Oprah Winfrey Show, November 27, 2002

Venus Williams's victory at Wimbledon in 2000 was the realization of a young girl's dream. Just 11 years before, as a wide-eyed nine-year-old, Venus visited tennis legend Chris Evert's home in Florida to admire her trophies, including the three Evert won at Wimbledon. The following year, Venus watched as Zina Garrison played the lawn courts of the famous event. Garrison was the first African American woman to play a Grand Slam final since Althea Gibson's historic 1957 championship match at Wimbledon. Years before she found herself on Centre Court, young Venus explained, "I'd like to win Wimbledon as many times as any one else can win it. More than any woman, man, or any junior did" (Jervis, 2002).

At age 20, Venus realized this dream and more when she defeated Lindsay Davenport in straight sets (6–3, 7–6). She was well aware of the history that had gone before her, as well as the history that she made with her championship win. Zina Garrison watched from the nearby guest box with Venus's younger sister Serena, both cheering her to victory. Althea Gibson, viewing the event from her home in East Orange, New Jersey, was likely cheering too. Gibson asked Garrison to pass on a word of advice to Venus before the historic match: "Bend your knees" (Wilstein, 2000). However, rather than make Venus nervous with this word from the legendary 72-year-old Gibson, Garrison decided to pass Venus a note instead. It read simply, yet profoundly, "The time is now" (Wilstein, 2000).

A Williams would hold Wimbledon victories for the next four years. Venus won in 2000 and 2001, followed by Serena, who defeated her sister for the title in 2002 and 2003. Few could dispute that this was their time. By 2004, the Williams sisters had been on the pro tennis circuit for only 10 years, yet they changed the face of professional women's tennis in countless ways. Venus began on the Women's Tennis Association (WTA) tour in 1994, with Serena following her older sister on the circuit a year later. Together they broke and set scores of records: fastest serves, gold medals at the 2000 U.S. Olympics in Sydney, Australia (one each for their doubles play, and one for Venus's singles play), first African American woman to hold the WTA number 1 ranking in more than 50 years (Venus), first duo to reach four straight Grand Slam doubles, and more. Record endorsement deals, art school, business, and celebrity came to the sisters as they forged new ground in the sport. They left their mark on sports history, and by their mid-twenties were poised to leave their mark on other venues as well.

Yet, by the time of the 2004 Wimbledon tournament, many wondered if their time in professional tennis had waned. Serena was destined to be called "gracious" rather than "victor" at Wimbledon when the 17-year-old Russian Maria Sharapova defeated her in 73 minutes in straight sets (6–1, 6–4). Although Serena Williams was favored to win the match, which was considered to be one of the most lopsided women's finals in more than a dozen years (Fendrich, 2004), she was unable to secure her third consecutive Wimbledon title. Sharapova was the 13th seed going into the tournament, the lowest seed to win since 1927 when Wimbledon began to seed its players. After the win, Sharapova told Williams, "I have to take this trophy from you for one year. I'm sorry" (Clarey, 2004). Williams told the crowd "It wasn't my day" after she congratulated Sharapova on Centre Court during the awards ceremony (Gordon, 2004). Serena's ranking dropped to 14th, putting her out of the top 10 for the first time in five years.

Venus, who still ranked 8th in the WTA when Wimbledon began, had not won a Grand Slam title in three years. Injuries, including a torn abdominal muscle and an injured ankle, contributed to her absence from the tennis court at major events throughout 2004. Then Venus was bounced out in Wimbledon's second round by Karolina Sprem (ranked 30th), her earliest exit from a Grand Slam tournament since her first-round loss at the French Open in 2001. The Wimbledon fall came amid controversy concerning an umpire's miscall that rewarded a point to Sprem, yet Venus recognized that this was not the sole cause of her loss. She told reporters, "I don't think one call makes a match," accepting her defeat with great composure and sportsmanship as she said of Sprem, "I just think she played really well, she deserved to win." Venus's ranking plummeted from 8 to 15 (Lusetich, 2004).

As tennis players, Venus and Serena received unprecedented media attention, caused debate as they stirred controversy, and captured the imagination of many children in inner cities and elsewhere. At the same time, there were some among the media who preyed on the prejudices and fears of those who felt the sisters had no place in the world of tennis. Few women of color had ever cracked the predominately white world of the WTA and professional tennis, and certainly none before them had accomplished as much as these sisters had. In 1949, just more than 50 years before Venus's win at Wimbledon, Althea Gibson became the first black female tennis player to compete in tournaments. During this time, tournaments were amateur play, and Gibson did not earn money for her participation. She played because she loved the sport and enjoyed the competition. In 1956, Gibson won the singles title at the French Open. In 1957, Gibson won Wimbledon, the first African American woman to do so. In 1958, Gibson won a second Wimbledon singles title, and she reached the finals of the U.S. Open, winning her first of two singles trophies for Grand Slam events. Competing in amateur tennis and later in professional golf, Gibson helped to break down racial barriers that were prominent during this time in U.S. history when civil rights and women's rights were foremost in the minds of many people. In part, Gibson's efforts and successes helped to pave the way for Venus and Serena.

Zina Garrison was one of the few African American women to play professional tennis in the years after Althea Gibson's reign. Though ranked 4th in the world, and named among the top 20 by the WTA for 14 years, she was still referred to as "the black American tennis player" (Aronson, 2001, p. 12). In 1996, she felt there were still many racial barriers that existed in the world of professional tennis. She worked to break down these barriers, urging Venus and Serena to win, and encouraging other inner-city youth to live full lives that included sports. She founded the Zina Garrison All Court Tennis Academy in Houston, Texas, to help other inner-city youth have the same opportunities that she had when she learned to play tennis as a 10-year-old through the MacGregor Park program in Houston.

Venus and Serena came to the tennis courts during a time when professional tennis generated unprecedented sums of money. However, it was not always this way. Lawn tennis games and tournaments had been played around the world since 1873, when Maj. Walter Clopton Wigfield designed the game to amuse guests at his manor at Nantclywd, Wales, and many tennis players, particularly those in major tournaments, were amateurs and did not play for money. In 1926, the first U.S. tennis players began to play for paying audiences; however, these professionals were not permitted to compete in the major tournaments with amateur players, much like the sport of ice skating remains to this day. Beginning in 1968, the Open era of tennis, this all changed. Any player could compete in the major tournaments, with many players beginning to make a living solely on their earnings from tennis (see Appendix A for a list of Grand Slam tournaments).

Following this Open era, Title IX of the Education Act of 1972 became law when President Richard Nixon signed the civil rights statute barring gender discrimination in education. Schools receiving federal funding of any kind were required to provide equal opportunities for girls to play sports as well as to provide adequate facilities for them. This federal act opened up many possibilities for girls in sports, and it contributed to breaking down some of the barriers and gender stereotypes about women athletes. Team and individual sports in high schools and universities changed dramatically, and girls began to compete more extensively than ever in organized and competitive games like soccer, field hockey, basketball, softball, track and field, gymnastics, and more. Many athletes, like U.S. soccer player Julie Foudy, attribute the success of women in sports in part to the possibilities afforded them through Title IX legislation. Researchers Leslie Heywood and Shari Dworkin noted that at the time Title IX legislation was enacted, only one in nine women participated in organized sports. By 2003, these numbers changed significantly: one in every 2.5 women competed in organized sports, with one third of all college women participating in competitive sports activities.

A year after Title IX was signed into law, tennis champion Billie Jean King, discouraged with the discrepancies between how men and women were treated in professional tennis, founded the WTA, becoming its first president. At the time, professional male tennis players were paid, on average, eight times more than women. A male tennis player might earn $12,500 for winning a tournament, whereas a woman might earn $1,500 (see http://www.wtatour.com). The WTA was the first successful tennis tour for women as it worked to bring more equality to the world of women's sports. In 1973, the U.S. Open became the first tournament to offer equal prize money for men and women.

By the time Venus and Serena entered the professional tennis circuit in the 1990s, women were being paid sums of money Althea Gibson and those tennis players of her era could never have imaged. In addition to the money professional women tennis players earned for tournament play, many received millions more for endorsements from major corporations like Reebok, Nike, Adidas, and others. In spite of these successes, many inequities and much gender bias still occurred against women in sports. In marking the 25th anniversary of Title IX legislation, then Secretary of Education Richard Riley noted some of the challenges that remained, including sexual harassment, unequal pay, and the fact that only one third of intercollegiate athletic scholarships were awarded to women. Although Riley noted the progress women had achieved in athletics, he believed there was still much work to do. In spite of the gains Title IX brought, it remained a controversial law that was threatened to be undone by President George W. Bush's Secretary of Education Rodney Paige's Commission on Opportunity in Athletics. Julie Foudy, captain of the U.S. National Women's Soccer Team, and Donna de Varona, a U.S. Olympic Champion in swimming, were members of the commission. They issued a minority report to explain their disagreement with key recommendations of the commission, and they established a Web site to "Save Title IX." Two key provisions of the report generated by the commission caused concern to Foudy and de Varona: (1) a provision that would allow Secretary of Education Paige to set a "reasonable variance" from the current Title IX standards for equality, and (2) allowing the secretary to explore "additional ways of demonstrating equity" (see http://www.savetitleix.com for more information). Because the language of the law was not specific about what equity meant or how the secretary would make decisions concerning the law, and because many myths remain about Title IX, including the myth that the law required quotas against men, Foudy and de Varona launched a public campaign to educate citizens about the law and to garner support in opposition to any proposed changes that would be detrimental to equal access to athletics for girls.

Although women had participated in professional and amateur sports for many decades prior to Title IX, they received minimal attention for their efforts until the 1990s, particularly when compared to men. Researchers Leslie Heywood and Shari Dworkin note that in a 20-year period before the 1990s, *Sports Illustrated* had only four covers featuring women athletes. This began to change in the 1990s, which Heywood and Dworkin refer to as a time when the image of the female athlete was new. This was due in part to the unprecedented participation and accomplishments of women in sports, as well as the attention they achieved as icons among the media. Gabrielle Reece, a volleyball superstar, model, and actress, was referred to as an "ubergirl" because she was big and strong and redefined the image of female athletes. Along with Reece, other women appeared powerful on the court or in their field of play, yet they appeared elegant and beautiful in other venues: track star Marion Jones, the 1999 U.S. women's soccer team, tennis player Anna Kournikova, and, of course, Venus and Serena Williams. In addition, Heywood and Dworkin suggested that offering up athletics as a solution to social problems suffered by women— including psychological and health problems associated with adolescent girls' self-esteem, depression, and breast cancer—was a new phenomenon, as was the idea that women participated and lived in the athlete's world. Female participation in sports was beginning to be seen as an expected occurrence rather than an exception engaged in by just a few women. These changes in women's participation in sport also raised questions around gendered understandings of male athletes: sacrificing oneself for the game, winner takes all, the athlete as hero, and the need to perform like a machine. Heywood and Dworkin pointed out how women's participation in sport complicates these traditionally male perceptions of athletics as women either adopt these ideas and/or insert their own perspectives on sport, particularly competitive sports. These developing understandings and evolving meanings of women in sport opened up new markets, new images, and new challenges for women athletes who were shaped not only by their physical activity but also by politics and culture. Venus and Serena Williams certainly contributed to these evolving images and understandings in unique and memorable ways through their incredible athleticism, their beauty and sense of style, and their intelligence and interest in life outside of the world of sports. Because of their unique contributions, this book will consider their lives, their accomplishments, and the challenges they face both on and off the court.

"YOU JUST CAN'T UNDERESTIMATE ANYONE"

After her Wimbledon defeat, Serena promised, "I'm definitely going to triple my efforts, do everything I can to play better next time.... Like I always say, everyone's a big threat. You just can't underestimate anyone" (Fendrich, 2004, p. B1). This statement, although directed toward Sharapova, could be applied to Serena and Venus as well. They are not to be underestimated, and their championships both on and off the tennis court have only begun. They provide hope, inspiration, and more to aspiring young athletes around the world. In order to begin to appreciate their influence, talent, and potential, it is important to understand where they came from and who their family is. The next chapter provides some background on the Williams family, beginning with the eccentric father of the tennis stars, Richard Williams, and their mother, Oracene Price.

Chapter 2

THE WILLIAMS FAMILY

The Williams family is perhaps the most talked-about family in the world of sports, and perhaps the most misunderstood as well. Theirs is a tight-knit and often private group that moves noticeably about in very public places. Tennis fans in the stands at Wimbledon, the U.S. Open, and other tournaments across the globe have witnessed the support they offer to one another and the tensions that accompany their presence at these very white, middle- and upper-class events. People notice and comment on their hair styles (particularly when Oracene had a bright orange Afro), their clothing, and their vocal participation in a sport characterized by long quiet moments as players rally. Most often, Venus and Serena are the only African Americans competing in major tennis tournaments, and their family and friends are the only people of color in the audience. Venus once commented on the impact of race on the Williams family's reputation: "It's not anyone's fault, but people just see black people in a different way, and they can't help it. They don't really understand us. We're a minority in this country. Most people don't grow up around blacks" (Aronson, 2001, p. 52).

Many people did not understand the Williams sisters because of their family, their race, and their religion. Because of this, the family faced much discrimination on the WTA circuit and elsewhere; however, Venus and Serena managed to achieve great success in the face of these misunderstandings and prejudices. Their accomplishments often are attributed to their father, whom they both admit has had an enormous influence on them, but their mother and siblings contributed a great deal to their successes as well.

MEET THE PARENTS:
RICHARD WILLIAMS AND ORACENE PRICE

I think people think I'm a genius. I think that those who thought I was crazy, I have never seen a black man come along that will speak his mind, hold his head up and say I just don't give a damn about what you think.

Richard Williams, *The Oprah Winfrey Show*,
November 27, 2002

Sports analysts scoffed at Richard Williams for coaching and managing his two daughters' tennis skills and careers. He never was trained formally in tennis, and he made what many experts considered to be unorthodox choices in coaching his daughters. In spite of the criticism directed toward him, Richard held fast to his convictions about what was best for the girls, and he never seemed to lose sight of his dreams. Because of this, some might call him visionary, whereas others would disregard him as crazy. Whatever the opinion might be, it was clear to anyone who listened to Richard talk about his life that he was driven to succeed, in large part because of his past.

Born on February 16, 1942, Richard Williams grew up poor in Shreveport, Louisiana. He was the only son of Julia Mae Williams, a single mother who had five children. According to Richard, his mother was a sharecropper who worked picking cotton to support her family. During the off-season, she found employment as a custodian at a local school. It is sometimes difficult to have an accurate picture of Richard's childhood and past, in part because he is known for telling stories that are wildly exaggerated. For example, writer L. Jon Wertheim noted that one of Richard's childhood friends, Arthur "Turd" Bryant, claimed that Richard's mother, nicknamed "Miss Knee," never grew cotton as Richard claimed. Wertheim further observed that Richard often told people he was a star high school athlete, but no record of this exists in the newspaper archives in Shreveport, and people who were involved in school athletics at the time Richard was in high school have no recollection of him. Many of the explanations Richard offered about his past have been questioned or disputed, and some are clearly untrue, adding to the curiosity and somewhat outrageous aura surrounding him.

As a young man, Richard helped his mother with her work and the family as well as he could. Richard claimed to have spent $150 of his own money as a young man to purchase the land where his family lived, and he reported that he built the family's small home with his own hands. Although on the outside the house had the appearance of modern amenities, including spigots and electrical wires, on the inside, it lacked running water and electricity. In a documentary on the Williams family, Richard is filmed revisiting this home, and he seemed to be clearly distraught at the extreme disrepair of the place (Jervis, 2002).

As a boy, Richard did not know his father well, and he admitted that his father rarely came to the family home, choosing instead to spend time with his girlfriend who lived down the street. The segregated South was not an easy place for young Richard to live, and his life was complicated by the fact that he did not have a father who was close to him. As a child, he witnessed many atrocities and experienced much loneliness. When he was six years old, young Richard watched helplessly as a white woman driving her car ran over his best friend from first grade as the child crossed the street to buy candy at the candy store. According to Richard, the woman never slowed down, and after she ran over his friend, she put the automobile in reverse, rolled down her window, and blamed the boy, telling those who would listen that he did not get out of her way. Then she drove callously away as the young boy died in the street. This had a tremendous impact on young Richard, and he later planted a tree in his yard because he felt lonely and needed to have something strong to nurture and to grow (Jervis, 2002).

Richard's mother encouraged him to get a good education so that he would not have to do the backbreaking work she did to eke out an existence. Because of his mother's influence, he likewise encouraged his own children to get a good education. After leaving high school, Richard moved to California to find work. He made his way to El Segundo, where he worked in a factory. There, he met Betty Johnson, whom he married in 1965. Together, they had two daughters and three sons. According to Wertheim (2002), Richard's oldest daughter, Sabrina, described the relationship between her mother and father as stormy and volatile. Their marriage ended in 1973.

It seems that Richard's tendency to spin tales had a long history. Sabrina recounted some of the difficulty she experienced as a young girl due to her father's storytelling. For instance, he once told her that he played professional basketball for the Los Angeles Lakers, but her friend's father had to tell her this was not true. Sabrina recalled that this "broke my heart. Richard—I don't call him my dad—is a manipulator. He likes to think he can make people believe what he wants them to" (Wertheim, 2002, p. 76).

During his years in California, Richard worked various jobs and then established his own security guard company, Samson Security, in the Watts section of Los Angeles. He also started other small businesses, including a telephone-book delivery service. Over the years, Richard had various business ventures, some that seemed outrageous (according to Rineberg [2003], Richard once claimed to own air space over India, and that people had to pay him money to fly through it) and others that seemed potentially lucrative. Indeed, at one time, Richard claimed to own 29 businesses that ranged from merchandizing and bottled water to publishing.

While living in Watts, Richard met Oracene Price (nicknamed Brandi), a nurse who attended the same church he did. Oracene was born in Saginaw, Michigan, the daughter of an automotive factory worker who moved from the Mississippi Delta to Detroit to find work. When Oracene met Richard, she already had graduated from Western Michigan University. As a young person, Oracene enjoyed sports, and she ran track and played basketball, volleyball, and baseball. She told reporter Roseanne Michie (2003) of *Tennis* magazine how Richard did not immediately believe her when she told him that she could hit a home run in baseball. One day as young Venus and Serena were practicing on the tennis court, Richard threw a tennis ball to Oracene and she hit it over the fence with a baseball bat. She said Richard was stunned.

Although there are some reports that Richard and Oracene married in 1972, Oracene explained that they did not marry until 1980, after Venus was born (Wertheim, 2002). The couple initially lived in Long Beach, California. When they married, Oracene already had three young daughters with Yusef A. K. Rasheed, who died before she married Richard Williams. Together, Richard and Oracene raised Oracene's three girls, Yetunde, Isha, and Lyndrea.

One day after watching a tennis match on television when Virginia Ruzici won $40,000, Richard claimed to develop a plan that is now legendary. Impressed by the amount of money Ruzici won from just a few days' play, he went home to his wife and said, "We gotta make two more kids" (Jervis, 2002). He told Oracene, "That's what I earn in a year! Let's put our kids in tennis so they can become millionaires" (Aronson, 2001, p. 19). Although Yetunde, Isha, and Lyndrea all had played tennis a bit as they were growing up, none were so interested in it that they would pursue a career in tennis. Yet, to Richard, nothing was out of reach if he worked hard enough and planned well enough. He began to study the game, reading magazines and watching instructional videos. His plan was to raise two children, who were yet unborn, to become tennis stars and to make a lot of money in the world of sports. Although no African American athlete had accomplished this in tennis before, he fully expected his own children would be successful in this pursuit. He noted, "There was a plan in effect two years before Venus was born." Richard considered himself to be a master planner, "I have a plan. I am a master planner. No one will out plan me" (Jervis, 2002). He proceeded to plan their tennis careers, their education, their diets, and more as he realized his dream of raising these young champions.

Oracene helped Richard to coach Venus and Serena, and her role included instilling in them a sense of pride and confidence. She explained, "Venus and Serena are assured in themselves, and that's something you have to make sure they have been taught since they were young. Self-confidence and self-esteem—if that's not embedded in them while they're young then they'll have doubts. It's important for them to be proud of who they are and not care what anyone says or how anyone tells them to act" (Michie, 2003).

Although Richard generally considered himself to be admired by others, noting that wherever he went, people looked up to him and said, "Oh that's Richards Williams," he always remembered his humble roots. In a 2002 interview, he explained, "I'm just a poor little cotton picker, that's all I'm gonna ever be. I don't want, wish to be anything else. I'm a great businessman too" (Jervis, 2002).

Not everyone shared Richard's appraisal of himself, and many in the press had difficulty making sense of his sometimes contradictory and seemingly exaggerated stories. Even a former hitting coach for Venus and Serena, Dave Rineberg, who was very close to the sisters through the 1990s, wrote of the difficulty he had understanding Richard's stories, explanations, and expectations (Rineberg, 2003).

In spite of the complicated stories Richard spun, Venus and Serena seemed to adore him and stand behind him, and they never publicly questioned his eccentricities. Venus explained that her father's childhood and history had a strong impact on her life. He raised them with family values that he learned while growing up in the Deep South in the 1950s, and he taught them to expect racism and to stand strong. He explained, "My kids today, they know the same traditions that I learned in the '40s and '50s about family, and that is why this family is so tight, so strong, so unique." He noted that if the family is seen at a tennis tournament and they are booed, it does not bother them because "we was taught for things like that many many years ago" (Jervis, 2002). Serena described her father by saying, "He's a great guy, and he's very nice. He's a comedian. We're both comedians. We love to tell jokes. He's very funny. He's super nice. He would go out of his way for anyone. He's a great coach. Take everything away from tennis, he's a great dad. He's very understanding. He doesn't put pressure on us to do anything. He's an unbelievable businessman. He's always thinking of creative ideas. I think that maybe people think differently. But I can't control what people think" (Chappell, 2002). Richard's son, Richard Jr., seemed to admire his father in much the same way Venus and Serena did. He explained, "I pick up a lot of my inspiration from my Dad, a lot of my courage comes through my Dad" (Jervis, 2002). His admiration for his father seemed clear when he explained that he could never fill his father's shoes (which are size 14).

In spite of his unconventional behavior, Richard Williams was considered by some to be a new role model for African American fathers. Lee Hubbard, of the Progressive Media Project, noted how Richard, like many other contemporary African American fathers, worked against stereotypes of black fathers as shiftless do-nothings who are not involved with their children (Hubbard, 2002). Family attorney Keven Davis observed that Richard raised his children to make decisions for themselves, but the children sought out Richard's council often because they knew how much he loved them (Jervis, 2002). However, these glowing accounts of Richard as a father seem to relay sentiments directed solely toward his relationship with his second family with Oracene and her daughters. According to Richard's oldest daughter, Sabrina, Richard turned his back on his first family, abandoning the five children he had with his first wife, Betty (Wertheim, 2002). When Richard left, Betty struggled financially, working two jobs to make ends meet. His sons spent time in the California prison system: Richard Jr. for a firearms offense, and Ronner for robbery (Wertheim, 2002). It is difficult to know how much Venus and Serena knew of this family, and it is difficult to speculate how these first five children's lives would have been different if their father had been involved with them to the degree that he was involved with Venus and Serena.

Richard and Oracene have had the unique experience of watching both of their youngest daughters achieve successes they may have never imagined, and they have been courtside as both women competed against one another during Grand Slam and tournament finals. Many people asked them how they handled this, which daughter they cheered for, and what potential damage this competition might have to their daughters' relationships. Oracene typically responded to such questions by explaining that she rooted for the daughter who was down, and that ultimately she was in the best position as their mother because they were all realizing their dreams. They all worked very hard and made sacrifices for Venus and Serena to be at the top of tennis. Oracene explained this to talk show host

Oprah Winfrey when she described how close her family was and how much they loved each other. She observed, "When I see them playing on the court and they're playing each other, I can't root for either one because I don't want either one to get mad at me ... especially Serena. Venus will be able to handle it, but Serena, no" (Harpo, 2002). She continued by saying that she did not want to see either daughter lose.

Richard and Oracene divorced in 2002, citing irreconcilable differences amid rumors of physical abuse. In spite of this separation in the family, they still worked together to coach and support their daughters, and they still emphasized and valued their family time. After the divorce, Venus and Serena were seen in public most often with their mother. When Oracene, Venus, and Serena spent time together, they were much like many mothers and daughters. They watched television and went out to dinner. They enjoyed one another's company and laughed a great deal together. Serena explained that they often made fun of their mother or shared a joke at her expense. "She's a good sport because if my kids mess with me as much as I mess with her, I don't know what I would do. But she's very easy-going. She's really great. She keeps us laughing, keeps us calm. She keeps us grounded" (*Ebony*, 2003, p. 156). Perhaps this was due in part to the balance between tennis and other aspects of life that Oracene tried to help the girls nurture. She explained, "Tennis can get one-dimensional. When we're on the court, we work hard and plan. But when we're not on the court, we don't talk about tennis. You need to have a life" (Michie, 2003).

Off the tennis court, Oracene worked with her various charity and foundation projects, including the OWL Foundation, which she founded to help children with learning disabilities to succeed in school. Serena also was involved with the OWL Foundation work. Oracene and her daughters also have worked to increase opportunities for children to play tennis in urban areas in the United States and at younger ages in Africa.

SISTER, SISTER

We often get the question: So how does it feel to have famous sisters? They're my sisters. I mean, we argue. We have disagreements. It's no different. I still see them as Venus Williams, Serena Williams, not Venus Williams, tennis star, not Serena Williams, tennis star.

Yetunde Price, *The Oprah Winfrey Show*,
November 27, 2002

Yetunde Hawanya Tara Price was the eldest of Oracene Price's five daughters. In 1991 when Richard and Oracene decided to relocate with Venus and Serena away from the dangerous neighborhood in Compton, California, so that the girls could have professional coaching in Florida, Yetunde opted to stay behind in the ghetto. Yetunde spent most of her life in Compton, a neighborhood made famous in films like *Boyz 'n the Hood* and *Menace II Society* as well as by notorious rap groups like NWA, known for pioneering gangsta rap in the 1980s. Yetunde had fallen in love with Jeffrey Johnson, a member of the dangerous Bloods gang, and she was going to have a child with him. She had begun her training as a nurse and wanted to make a life where she was. After her first son, Jeffrey Jr., was born, Johnson was arrested and put in jail for assaulting a police officer and taking a car without consent. Yetunde then met Byron Bobbitt, and the two married in Las Vegas. Bobbitt had a criminal record for drugs and firearms convictions, and Yetunde's life with him allegedly was filled with violence. Even Jeffrey Johnson's sister, one of Yetunde's friends, observed that "Yetunde seemed to be addicted to dangerous types. I guess she just liked a certain type of man: strong and dominant" (*Ithaca Times*, 2004).

As Venus and Serena earned wealth and fame, their lifestyles greatly contrasted with that of their oldest sister. Yetunde struggled to make ends meet and to provide for her children while she worked as a nurse, caring for people in their homes. She later established her own hair salon, called Headed Your Way, with a friend from high school. Yet, in spite of their different lifestyles and economic resources, Yetunde remained very proud and supportive of her famous little sisters, and she was never envious. In fact, Yetunde reportedly insisted on paying her own airfare when she traveled as a personal assistant to Venus and Serena's tennis tournaments. In a celebratory and glamorous moment, Yetunde accompanied her sister Serena to the Kodak Theater in Hollywood for the 11th Annual ESPY Awards on July 16, 2003. They were photographed together after the ceremony as Serena smiled and held her award for best female athlete.

As she became more financially secure, Yetunde moved 40 miles north of the ghetto with her three children to live in Corona. She thought the schools in Corona would be better for her children, and the neighborhood would be safer. Yet, she sometimes felt out of place in her new, mostly white neighborhood, and so she still visited Compton and her old friends frequently. One visit to the old neighborhood, however, culminated in tragedy during the early morning hours of September 14, 2003, when Yetunde was murdered by someone wielding an AK-47. This supposedly random shooting happened on the 1100 block of East Greenleaf Boulevard while Yetunde was sitting in her white SUV with a friend named Rolland Wormley. When Wormley realized Yetunde had been shot, he drove her to his mother's house in Long Beach, where he called police, and then he took her to Long Beach Memorial Hospital, where she died. Yetunde Price was 31 years old.

On January 20, 2004, the Los Angeles County District Attorney's office announced that Robert Edward Maxfield, a 23-year-old Southside Crips gang member, and Michael Hammer, a 24-year-old Crips member, had been charged with murder in Yetunde Price's death. Maxfield, who later pled not guilty to the charges, also was accused of attempting to murder Rolland Wormley, Yetunde's friend who was driving her vehicle when she was killed. Although Wormley was not a suspect in Yetunde's murder, he also was charged as a result of events that evening, including parole violation and assault with a deadly weapon.

At the time of Yetunde's death, Venus was in New York and Serena was in Toronto filming a television drama series. The entire family immediately traveled to California, and they issued a statement that said, "We are extremely shocked, saddened, and devastated by the shooting death of our beloved Yetunde. She was our nucleus and our rock. She was personal assistant, confidant, and adviser to her sisters, and her death leaves a void that can never be filled. Our grief is overwhelming, and this is the saddest day of our lives."

Some critics wondered if this tragic loss was too much for Venus and Serena to bear, and some speculated that the sisters might leave tennis for good in the wake of their grief. Not only did the family experience tremendous devastation after Yetunde's death, they also had difficult decisions to make about how to best care for Yetunde's three children, which resulted in a bitter custody suit over Jair (6 years old at the time of the custody suit), Justus (10 years old), and Jeffrey (12 years old). Oracene wanted to care for the children, and the children were seen at tennis tournaments around the world with their famous aunts. Her efforts to care for the children and the corresponding bitter custody battle must have been difficult for the entire family to bear. In fact, Oracene traveled to a Los Angeles court on June 24, 2004, while Venus and Serena were playing at Wimbledon, in order to secure permanent custody of the three children. The father of the oldest child, Jeffrey, agreed to the custody arrangement because he recognized that the Williams family would be able to provide experiences and safety to young Jeffrey that he could not. He told the

Ithaca Times (2004), "I just want what's best for my son JJ. Here, the 13-year-olds are into gangs and crack cocaine. In Corona, they have the best schools in the state, PlayStation and sports. With them [the Williams family], he'll travel in style to France, Spain, England. How can I deprive him of that opportunity? In any case, I can see him whenever I choose." However, Jair and Justus's father saw things differently. Byron Larry Bob-bitt, who is alleged to have stalked and threatened Oracene, felt that his children were brainwashed by the Williams family after Yetunde's death and that the Williams family was unfit to keep the children.

On November 5, 2004, a judge declared a mistrial in the case against Aaron Michael Hammer, one of two men accused of shooting Yetunde Price. The jury voted 9–3 in favor of acquitting Hammer after prosecutors explained that the bullet that killed Yetunde was not from Hammer's gun. Even though California law allows someone to be prosecuted for murder for taking part in a crime in which someone was killed, it was not clear to jurors what Hammer's involvement in the crime had been even though, hours after the shooting, Hammer admitted to firing six shots at Yetunde's SUV. It was supposedly gang member Robert Edward Maxfield's gun that delivered the fatal shot as he defended a crack house in the Compton neighborhood, but jurors were unable to deliver a guilty verdict in his case either. Just days after the Hammer case ended in a hung jury, a separate jury delivered a mistrial in the Maxfield case. Five members of the jury wanted to convict Maxfield, whereas six wanted to acquit him, and one could not decide.

Venus and Serena's other older sisters, Isha and Lyndrea, largely have stayed out of the public eye. Isha, who played tennis in college, went to law school in Washington, whereas Lyndrea, who also played tennis in college, worked as a Web designer, actress, and singer. When she appeared with her sisters on *The Oprah Winfrey Show*, Lyndrea emphasized that the sisters were all very ambitious, spiritual, and family-oriented people (Harpo, 2002).

Before Yetunde's death, the sisters communicated, as many sisters do, on a daily basis. Isha described their relationship by telling Oprah that the sisters were very close and that each day one of them has talked with at least one other sister. She went on to say, "We talk about everything, about life issues, about men, about world issues, you know, just every-thing.... I think it is one of the greatest things in the world to have sis-ters.... [W]omen out there who have sisters are so blessed, because there's nothing like it" (Harpo, 2002). Their shared loss and grief over Yetunde's death would no doubt change their relationships and their lives in pro-found ways. They had one another to lean on, to be sure, and they had their religious beliefs to help them through the difficult times following Yetunde's death.

TAKING IT TO THE STREETS: THE JEHOVAH'S WITNESS RELIGION

Oracene and her daughters are Jehovah's Witnesses, a religion that contributed in unique ways to their tight family bonds. The Williams family is not the first celebrity family to call attention to this faith. The Jackson family and the Wayans family, including actor brothers Keenan, Shawn, Damon, and Marlon, are also Jehovah's Witnesses.

The Jehovah's Witnesses began as an organized group in the 1870s in Allegheny, Pennsylvania, under the leadership of Charles Taze Russell. Jehovah's Witnesses believe in God, whom they refer to as Jehovah, as the almighty creator of the heavens and the Earth. They also believe that the Earth will remain forever and that all people, living and dead, who fit into God's plan for the Earth will live on it eternally. Serena shared the importance of spirituality and what her religion meant to her: "I'm a Jehovah's Witness. If you don't believe in God—I think if you don't believe in God, it's going to be tough to live life because pretty much that's the basis of life, it comes from God. And so being a Jehovah's Witness, obviously we believe in God and the Bible. And without Him, I wouldn't be here right now. I really thank Him for everything. I've been blessed, really. People are sick, just born with just disorders, and I've been blessed to be born, you know, pretty much healthy" (ASAP Sports, Serena Williams, July 6, 2002).

The Jehovah's Witnesses are part of a worldwide organization with more than six million members who study the Bible, believing it is God's word and the truth. As a group, Jehovah's Witnesses do not believe in participating in politics or wars, and they do not believe in the pursuit of excessive wealth, prominence, or pleasure. In addition, they do not celebrate holidays that have non-Christian religious origins or national ties, like the Fourth of July, Labor Day, or Memorial Day. Because Jehovah's Witnesses believe that they should show allegiance only to God, they do not vote, pledge allegiance to the flag, or participate in military duty. In spite of the typically apolitical stance that characterizes Jehovah's Witnesses, Serena did publicly express an opinion concerning the use of the Confederate flag. In April 2000, she withdrew from the Family Circle Cup tournament in support of the NAACP's boycott of the Confederate flag and its use in South Carolina, where the tournament was being held.

The Witnesses gather for weekly Bible meetings, they read and study teachings and publications from the Watchtower Organization, and they witness to others about their religion. This means that they spend time telling other people about their religion. Venus and Serena have gone door-to-door distributing pamphlets and information about their religion, and they sometimes publicly discuss their religion and misconceptions people have about it. Both Venus and Serena have commented in interviews that many people do not understand their religion, just as many often do not understand the Williams family, characterizing them as unsociable or unfriendly. Jehovah's Witnesses believe, among other things, that Christians should remain separate from the world. This may contribute in part to the fact that the Williams family is sometimes perceived to be aloof from others, particularly on the WTA Tour. As Serena explained to *Ebony* magazine, her association with other tennis players stays primarily on the court. "I wouldn't say we are friends.... I don't go out to dinner with them, to the movies. But I'm cordial. I say, 'Hi, how are you doing'" (Chappell, 2002). Jehovah's Witnesses often are encouraged to have friends and to socialize only with others who share their religious beliefs.

FAMILY TIES

In all, it is difficult to understand Venus and Serena without knowing something about their family and their beliefs. Their beliefs have been shaped in part by their father and his experiences growing up in the Deep South before the civil rights movement and by their mother, who encourages and supports them both on and off the tennis courts. Their tight bonds with their mother and sisters has been forged through good times and bad as they shared the economic difficulties of their childhood in Compton, the victories of their tennis careers, and the tragic loss of Yetunde. Through it all, their religion has played a key role, grounding them in their commitments to one another. The Williams family is very close and no doubt will remain so whatever the future may hold.

Chapter 3

VENUS

The music-box tune from an ice-cream truck making its way through the streets of Compton, California, summoned young Venus Williams to its door. Dreamsicles, Eskimo Pies, ice-cream sandwiches, and the promise of other cold, sweet treats enticed the pigtailed youngster as she took a break from the tennis court to indulge in some refreshing reward. She often spent her entire allowance at the ice-cream truck, and of course, as the older sister, she was always willing to share with her younger sister, Serena, who was never far behind. Serena always needed to have what Venus had, and ice-cream treats would be no exception.

As a child, Venus kept a special, watchful eye on her little sister. They were growing up in a tough neighborhood, and Venus had to look out for Serena. Venus walked her sister to her kindergarten class each day, staying long enough to be sure that Serena was going to be fine. And one Wednesday, when Serena forgot her lunch money, Venus thought nothing of giving hers away. Venus told her, "Well, Serena, you take my money. You go eat. I won't eat." Venus went without her lunch, and sometimes without her coat just to make sure her sister was all right. These were moments they laughed about as they grew older, but they demonstrate well how Venus always considered her sister first. "If she needs something taken care of, I'm the one," Venus explained (Olson, 2002).

Her tendency to take special care of Serena continued as they later competed in tennis. When Serena defeated Venus to win Wimbledon in 2002, Venus quietly reminded her sister to curtsy during the trophy presentation (Olson, 2002). After losing a match to Serena at the 2002 U.S.

Open, Venus graciously explained, "I think Serena was the best player in the tournament this year" (Olson, 2002). Some critics would accuse Venus of throwing a match to Serena, but Venus had a competitive spirit on the court and the drive always to play her best game. She would give her sister anything, except a match. But when Serena did win, Venus was genuinely happy for her as she planned how to improve for the next match.

Venus would have shared anything with any of her sisters, and she would look out for all of them the best she could. Although she was not the oldest of her mother's five daughters, she was considered to be the oldest in spirit and was protective of her sisters. It was just her nature. Her sisters all came to her for advice, and she counseled them in ways on which they grew to rely and trust. Her sister Isha said that Venus had "an old soul" (Harpo, 2002).

This "old soul" would grow up to take on serious challenges that would try her strength and resolve, and she would see her sisters and her family through difficult times and through triumphs. She would change the face of women's tennis, leaving her mark on sports history before she reached 20 years of age. But tennis was not the only thing in her life. Much more engaged young Venus Williams, and she had many more facets to her life than sport.

EARLY DAYS

The name Venus comes from the Roman goddess of love and beauty, and across the ages it has been the name of the brightest planet in our solar system, the name of famous sculptures and paintings, the name of the Wimbledon trophy (called the Venus Rosewater), and now the name of a celebrity tennis player. Venus Ebony Starr Williams was born on June 20, 1980, in Lynwood, California, Richard Williams's and Oracene Price's oldest child together, and Oracene's fourth daughter. Shortly after Venus was born, her family moved to Michigan, where her mother had been raised, and it was there that Venus's younger sister Serena was born. Yet, not long after her sister's birth, the family returned to California to make a home in the ghetto. Their father later explained that he wanted them to grow up in the ghetto so that they would understand the need for a good education, the need to have a different life. Living in the ghetto was Richard Williams's way of teaching his girls a tough lesson. He explained, "I wanted to live in the worst ghetto in the world so they could see all the bad that could happen to you if you don't get an education" (Clarke, 2003). When the two sisters began to earn wealth and fame, he often referred to them as the ghetto Cinderellas.

As a young child, Venus always seemed to have a serious disposition, and she often appeared to be lost in thought. Her mother characterized her as "deep" and recalled how she would watch young Venus while she sat in her chair as a baby. Oracene thought little Venus would be dreaming, and Oracene would wonder, "What in the world is this little girl thinking about?" (Harpo, 2002). As Venus grew up, she retained her contemplative spirit, becoming an avid reader and researcher. The Bible was her favorite book, but she always loved to study new subjects and learn new things. In fact, Venus's elementary school teachers sometimes wondered about her. "They would say I was reading too many books in class, not paying attention to the lesson, that I could do a lot better, but I daydreamed too much," Venus explained (ASAP Sports, Venus Williams, June 28, 2000). In spite of this serious side, Venus enjoyed a good laugh and was always ready to share a joke with her sisters and her mother.

Venus began to play tennis as a very young child when her father took her to the tennis courts in Compton, California. The four-year-old loved tennis as soon as she held a racquet in her hand. She returned volley after volley to her Dad as he served hundreds of balls to her from a grocery store cart, and she often would cry when it was time to go home. At one point, Richard even took her tennis racquet from her for a year because he feared she loved the game too much. This began the trend of on-again off-again

---

Events of 1980

Hewlett Packard released its first personal computer.

U.S. President Jimmy Carter announced that the United States would boycott the Olympic Games in Moscow.

Mount St. Helens erupted in Washington State, killing 57 people.

Saddam Hussein was elected president of Iraq.

The Iran-Iraq War began.

Ronald Reagan won the United States presidential election.

John Lennon was shot and killed in New York City on December 8.

CNN was launched.

Also born in 1980: Michelle Kwan, Chelsea Clinton, Jessica Simpson, Macaulay Culkin, Yao Ming, and Martina Hingis.

time with tennis. Tennis would not be the only thing in her life. Richard made sure of this. He always wanted Venus to have other interests, to be well balanced, and, most importantly, to have a good education. In fact, there were times when Venus would not be permitted to practice, even after she was a well-known champion, if Richard felt her grades in school were not as high as they should be.

At 14, Venus turned pro against her father's wishes. In 1995, the WTA rules were changing in light of criticism about age and the amount of play athletes could engage. In part, this had to do with controversy surrounding young players, including Tracey Austin, a tennis prodigy plagued by injury at an early age, and, more recently, Jennifer Capriati, who turned pro at age 13 but then left the tennis scene amid turmoil. In 1990, Capriati burst onto the professional circuit, becoming the youngest player ever to reach a professional tennis final when she competed in her first pro match in Boca Raton, Florida. She won an Olympic gold medal in 1992 when she defeated Steffi Graf in Barcelona, Spain. In spite of her success on the court, Capriati experienced personal trouble off the court. In 1993, she was arrested on charges of shoplifting from a jewelry store, although she was not prosecuted. Then in May 1994, Capriati faced drug possession allegations. She was never formerly charged, but she did enter a drug rehabilitation program in Miami, Florida, later that same year. By 1995, Capriati was reportedly burned out and she temporarily abandoned tennis. Since that time, she has experienced a remarkable comeback, achieving a number 1 ranking from the WTA in October 2001. By the time Capriati returned to the game, however, the WTA rules had changed for younger players. Beginning in 1995, players would need to be 16 years old in order to turn professional, and they would be permitted to play only a limited number of tournaments until they reached 18. In 1994, Venus needed to decide whether to turn pro right away before the WTA rules change took effect or to wait until she was older to play on the pro circuit. The Williams family took a vote, but Richard abstained in protest. Venus made her professional debut in 1994, winning her first match against Shaun Stafford at the Bank of the West Classic in Oakland, California.

When she began her play with the WTA tour, Venus was still in high school, balancing her classes with tennis practice and tournament play. By the time she was 17, she worked on completing her high school requirements and added some college classes to the mix: political science, freshman communications, and cohesive writing. She put in a tough year juggling her education and her tennis responsibilities. As she described it, "It wasn't easy. I would have to stay up late at night and write reports. I couldn't even type. I had to type my own. It was just a lot of work" (ASAP Sports, Venus Williams, August 25, 1997).

Venus graduated from the Driftwood Academy in Lake Park, Florida, in 1997, two years after entering the professional tennis circuit, bringing to a close the first phase of her education, which included a mixture of public, private, and home schooling experiences. Math was never Venus's favorite subject, but she excelled in all other areas of her study, earning better than a 3.0 grade point average upon her graduation. After her high school graduation, Venus completed classes at the Art Institute in Florida and then went on to earn a certificate in interior design from Palm Beach Community College. To complete the requirements for this certificate, Venus took courses that taught her about color, design, the history of interior design, and more. She did the majority of her course work during the 11-week fall semester, between October and December each year, and through online study. The school did not make special exceptions for Venus, so if she was playing tennis, she needed to arrange it around her school schedule and online course work. After completing her certificate, she continued her education by studying for a bachelor's degree in interior design.

TYPICAL DAYS (CIRCA 2004)

Venus, nicknamed "V," "VW," "V-Dub," or "Dub," woke up on typical mornings in time to be on the tennis court between 8 and 9 A.M., although she claimed she did not like to wake too early. Each morning, she played tennis for about two hours, followed by fitness training and physical therapy. The fitness training helped her strength and endurance on the court, and the physical therapy helped to heal injuries and to prevent future injuries. She ran, biked, or worked out, sometimes with Thera-Bands, to increase her strength, even though she did not like to go to the gym all that much. Unfortunately, a pulled abdominal muscle and a wrist injury sidelined Venus for a time in 2003 and 2004.

Each Tuesday, Venus had guitar lessons. She claimed that Serena inspired her to begin to play the guitar again after a six-year hiatus from the instrument. When Serena returned from a trip with a brand new guitar, Venus knew she had to have one too. Venus shopped around and found a guitar she fell in love with, and she named her guitar Baby Jamie. Jamie is a Taylor 410-ce, an acoustic/electric guitar. Venus also played the bass guitar, but she had not given her bass guitar a name. She could play well enough to play some of her favorite songs on Baby Jamie: "Fly Away," by

Lenny Kravitz, and "Amber" by 311. The band 311, whose five members were from Nebraska, was her favorite, with their unique blend of rap and rock. Venus found the band's music to be deep, moving, and fun, and she liked the way they experimented with sound. One memorable highlight of 2004 was when Venus was in Tokyo for the Toray Pan Pacific Tournament. Although she had to withdraw from the tournament because of an injury, she was able to meet 311 and see them in concert.

Each Friday, Venus had a Spanish class. Venus studied and spoke several languages, including French, Italian, and Russian, and she reportedly devoured language tapes as she attempted to master the pronunciation, intonation, and nuances of the languages she studied (Tresniowski and Rozsa, 2004). Her language study was put to good use when she traveled abroad. One particularly notable moment came when she won the French Open. Venus pleasantly surprised the crowd when she graciously accepted her trophy in French, something she aspired to do from the time she was a child. Serena explained to Oprah Winfrey how impressed she and Venus were when they watched someone win the French Open and then speak in French. She explained that they both decided that when they went to the French Open, they would both be able to do the same thing (Harpo, 2002).

After tennis and her various classes and lessons, Venus spent most of her day at the office of her interior design firm, V Starr Interiors, which she established in 2002. Venus worked on design projects, reviewed the accounts and numbers for the business, and planned for the future as she oversaw the general operations of the business, making certain things were running efficiently and well. It took a great deal of her time, particularly in the years when she started her business. During a visit with Oprah Winfrey in 2002, Venus explained how she was working overtime on the business, doing everything from writing the brochures to getting the various licenses she needed. She wanted the business to be successful, and she knew the first months were critical. Even Venus's mother worried that she was working too hard, but once she was able to hire some staff to help her with the work, it became a bit easier.

In her free time, Venus studied, mostly fashion, languages, and the Bible. She also liked to hang out with Bob, her pet Yorkie, as she watched television, including her favorite show *The Golden Girls*, or played video games and Game Boy. Venus enjoyed art, especially that of young emerging artists, and she appreciated the styles of artists all around the world. She was particularly drawn to Asian antiques. Venus liked to write poetry, something she began to do when she was in her teens, and she hoped to publish a book of poetry some day. In 2004, Venus became a published author when *How to Play Tennis: Learn How to Play the Williams Sisters'*

Way, the book she coauthored with her sister Serena, landed in bookstores around the world. As this book went to press, she began to work on a second book that offered sisterly advice for young girls.

NOT SO TYPICAL DAYS, TYPICALLY

When she traveled to play in tournaments, Venus was able to rest. Even though the typical pressure came with anticipating each match, her time away from home was much less busy than her time at home. The days when she did not have matches began much the same way as her days at home: tennis and fitness training. On days when she was playing a match, she usually hit for about two hours in the morning so that she was warmed up and ready to play. She preferred to play matches during the day. Evening matches required her to sit around the hotel as she waited for game time, something Venus did not like too much.

When visiting a new city, Venus always tried to take in as many of the sights as her schedule would allow, even though it was sometimes hard to fit in extra touring and shopping during busy tournaments. When she was in Warsaw, Poland, in 2003, she visited the zoo and the old city. In February 2004, while she was in London, Venus attended the Elle Style Awards, the Brits (a music award show), and some other fashion shows. Luckily for Venus, she was in London during Fashion Week, and she was able to glimpse the latest styles and trends. She also attended a N.E.R.D. concert, and she met female rap artist Missy Elliott and John and Simon from the 1980s band Duran Duran. Usually when Venus was in London, she needed to spend most of her time at Wimbledon. For this visit, she was glad to be able to see the city and enjoy the fashion and music.

OTHER SPORTS

Venus is a talented athlete, and tennis is not the only sport she has played. As a youngster, she practiced gymnastics and dance, and before she was 10 years old, Venus showed tremendous promise running track. She was particularly strong at sprinting and mid-distance events. She won 19 straight meets, running the mile in 5 minutes 29 seconds as an eight-year-old (see Puma, 2001). When asked by a reporter at the 1998 U.S. Open, "Do you think you could have excelled at any sport that you wanted to?" Venus replied, "I think so. But I think tennis is the best because you have the opportunity to have a large income, you travel the world. I think it's the best women's sport as far as notoriety. It really is. I like it" (ASAP Sports, Venus Williams, September 7, 1998).

In addition to playing sports, Venus is a sports fan. She has attended Miami Heat basketball games, and she particularly liked the Florida Marlins. At times, she has been spotted in the stands at Marlins games when they played at home in Miami. In 2003, Venus and Serena both attended some of the World Series to watch the Marlins. Pitcher Dontrelle Willis was one of their favorite players. Venus threw an opening pitch to Willis on October 11, 2003, when the Marlins faced Chicago in the National League Championship series. Willis dropped his glove and hugged Venus after he caught the pitch, and Sammy Sosa came from the dugout to greet her.

After she retires from professional tennis, Venus would like to continue her career in interior design and fashion design, and she might like to take up choreography and music production. Whereas sister Serena has a clear interest in acting, Venus sees herself more as a "behind-the-scenes girl" (Tresniowski & Rozsa, 2004).

PRIVATE LIFE, PUBLIC MISUNDERSTANDINGS

Venus is considered to be kind and generous by those who are closest to her, but she is sometimes depicted as cold or arrogant in the media and popular press. This may be due in part to a perception that she achieved too much as a woman in sports, or perhaps because of her race, misunderstandings about her religious beliefs, or some combination of these factors. Sometimes she is called arrogant when she refuses to answer a reporter's question. Other times she is labeled as arrogant because she does not socialize with other female tennis players on the tour. Chandra Rubin, who was her doubles partner at the 2004 Olympics in Athens when Serena withdrew because of a knee injury, and Alexandra Stevenson, both African American players, are the only players she does socialize with.

One of Venus's more outspoken critics is fellow competitor Lindsay Davenport. She said of Venus and her family: "Who knows what's going on with that family. Serena's more friendly. At least she can bring herself to say hi. Venus can't—or won't—even speak. Venus likes to give the impression that she's so great, that she's 'Da Bomb,' or whatever. She can say it all she wants but that just means she doesn't have it. She gets psyched out in big matches. She's not happy with her sister winning and the pressure is really falling on her" (Wertheim, 2002, p. 14).

Similarly, former tennis champion and now sports commentator John McEnroe has offered negative statements about Venus in public venues. McEnroe has accused Venus of having no respect for anyone in the game, for having no humility, and for not saying hello to people in the locker room. Although some find it odd that this former "bad boy" of tennis would offer such statements given his past behavior on and off the tennis court, Venus has been known to reply simply and directly in response to questions about McEnroe's criticisms of her: "I've never had a conversation with [McEnroe] ... he doesn't know me" (Cortez, 2000).

In spite of these disapprovals from others, Venus is often her own worst critic. However, even after a tough match or a disappointing loss, she tries to focus on the future as she works to improve her game yet keep tennis in perspective. A good example of this came in July 2004 when Venus returned to compete at the Bank of West Classic, the event at which she made her professional debut but lost in the finals to Arantxa Sanchez-Vicario 10 years earlier. After winning the second round of the tournament, which came shortly after her early defeat at Wimbledon, Venus, who was the number 1 seed, explained: "The problem is sometimes I'm actually too hard on myself.... You shouldn't dwell on the bad moments, especially since there's been so many. I had been thinking about each and every error as if it's monumental and life-threatening, which it isn't" (Tresniowski and Rozsa, 2004).

Venus describes herself differently than her critics would. "I have an aggressive style of play, but as a person I'm pretty gentle" (Jervis, 2002). She remains very private about much of her personal life, including her personal relationships, particularly with men. She has been romantically linked for several years to David Tomassoni, a former bodyguard who is now a clothing company executive. Whereas he calls himself Venus's special friend, in public she has said nothing of their relationship.

"I HAD A GREAT TIME"

In Compton, California, Serena once admired a gold trophy Venus won, so Venus gave it to her, claiming that she liked the color silver better (Olson, 2002). Although she maintained that her most memorable career moment was being in the 2000 Olympic Games, where she won gold medals for her singles play as well as for her play with sister Serena in the doubles tournament, Venus loaned her gold medals to Serena for a photo shoot after Serena misplaced her own. Like days gone by, Venus continued to be there for her sister as they grew into adulthood, giving Serena anything she needed.

After the 2000 Wimbledon, when Venus defeated Serena in the semifinals, a reporter asked what feelings she had about playing on the most celebrated court in the world after beginning so humbly on a hard neighborhood court in California. Venus replied, "You know, it's my life. The whole time I've had a great time, I've had a great life. I haven't had a lot of problems. Sure, you know, maybe living in Compton isn't like the most desired place to live, not in the Top 100. But I had a great time. I still miss the ice cream trucks" (ASAP Sports, Venus Williams, July 6, 2000).

Chapter 4

SERENA

I'm not a tennis superstar. I'm a superstar.
Serena Williams, July 4, 2004, World Tennis Network

As the U.S. Open was getting under way at New York City's Flushing Meadows Corona Park during the late summer of 2004, Serena Williams was in her favorite position, the center of attention. To begin, there were many questions about her health and her ability to compete in the tournament. Just a month earlier, she withdrew from the U.S. Olympic team three hours before the plane was set to depart for Athens, Greece. Although she had knee surgery nearly a year prior to this event, her injury had not healed to the degree that doctors had hoped, and she was advised not to play tennis in the Olympic Games. On August 11, 2004, Serena spent the morning before her scheduled flight on the talk-show circuit to discuss her pending play in the Olympics. She visited the *Today Show*, followed by *Regis and Kelly*. Serena told talk-show hosts Kelly Ripa and Bryant Gumbel (who was sitting in for Regis Philbin) how a second gold medal would mean more to her than winning a Grand Slam event. However, just hours later, her story changed. After a visit to Dr. David Altchek, a specialist who examined her knee, Serena withdrew from the Olympics. Altchek's advice was consistent with that of other doctors who told her throughout the summer that continued play on her knee would risk more serious damage. Earlier in the summer, Serena had to withdraw from the Acura Classic in San Diego, where she reinjured her knee, and then from the Rogers Cup in Montreal. Stepping away from the Olympics, however, was the biggest personal letdown for Serena. She released a statement to explain her decision: "I am sad and disappointed, not only because I am unable to travel to Greece and participate in the Olympics, but also because I gave my word that I would play. I feel that I am letting down my sister, Venus, Zina Garrison, and the other members of the U.S. Tennis team by not participating. I have been advised that by playing, I could cause long-term damage to my knee. I want to thank my fans, the USTA, the United States Olympic Committee, and the American people for your support. I will be cheering on our team, wishing I were there. I will starting extensive rehabilitation immediately, and look forward to coming back stronger than ever very soon" (Bohnert, 2004). These withdrawals and cancellations were fresh in the minds of tennis fans and the press as Serena began to compete in the U.S. Open, and many wondered if her knee could withstand the rigorous tournament play.

In addition to speculation about her health, Serena generated a great deal of attention with her clothing. Just prior to the tournament, she released a new line of tennis outfits she designed for Nike. Serena debuted the line at the U.S. Open when she appeared for her first match in a denim tennis skirt, a black studded tank top, a matching denim jacket with a rhinestone studded "SERENA" on the back, and black knee-high "boots" (a Lycra legging that zipped off her legs when she was ready to play). She described her choice of clothing as her "rebel" look, explaining that she would prefer to look good rather than to be comfortable. Major news media, from the *New York Times* and *Washington Post* to the Xinhua News Agency in China, reported extensively on this outfit and the others that followed, including a micromini skirt she wore during her second round. There was no question about it, Serena was a star.

It was not until Serena reached the quarterfinals that attention really began to shift from her health and clothing to her tennis playing. The quarterfinal match against Jennifer Capriati was intense and controversial. Serena played well throughout the first set, winning 6–2. Then she began to make a series of unforced errors, and umpire Mariana Alves overruled a call by a line judge, giving a point to Capriati. Serena questioned the umpire in uncharacteristic form, but she did not push for the tournament referee to intervene. By that point, the momentum had turned, and although Serena played a tough match, it was hard for her to shake the bad call and the potential for more to come. After the match, Serena told reporters she felt very angry and bitter, but she admitted that her loss came because she just "didn't play right" (Robertson, 2004). She vowed to return to the U.S. Open the next year. After all, she was still a tennis superstar.

Although the U.S. Open did not end as Serena would have liked, there was no question about the dominance she still retained in the sport and the attention she earned through her other interests, including clothing design and acting. She was not going to shrink away from the game, and she was not about to give up her other interests either. She would do both. Serena left the U.S. Open with a renewed commitment to succeed. She explained, "I consider myself the best right now even though I haven't won a Grand Slam this year, I've competed in three. I always consider myself the best. Not only on the court, but off the court I always try to have a great attitude, win, lose or draw. It's a game. I'll be here next year. I'll play a tournament next week" (ASAP Sports, Serena Williams, September 7, 2004).

A STAR IS BORN

Serena Jameka Williams (nicknamed "Meeka") was born on September 26, 1981, in Saginaw, Michigan, a town 90 miles north of Detroit and 20 miles from Saginaw Bay on Lake Huron. The Saginaw River runs through the center of town, but Saginaw is the only county in the state of Michigan without a natural lake.

Whereas Venus's role in the Williams family seemed to be that of caretaker and sage, Serena's seemed to vacillate between that of admirer and princess. As the youngest in the family, Serena looked up to her older sisters. She tried to be just like Venus and her older sister Lyndrea, and she sometimes thought she was Venus when she was little. "I was Venus ... there were two Venus Williams in the Williams family... It was really tough for me to finally stop being Venus and become the person who I am, Serena," she explained (Harpo, 2002). When Serena was a child, her parents would even make her order her meal first when they went to a restaurant. If they did not insist on this, then Serena would order just what Venus did. The problem was, even when they did insist on Serena ordering first, she would change her mind after Venus ordered.

As "princess," Serena's favorite thing to do was to look at herself and to have others look at her. Her mother explained, "Serena is outgoing. She's very flashy. She's a little too flashy for me.... But she loves Serena. And she'll tell you that. One of her hobbies is looking in the mirror" (Harpo, 2002). Serena told talk show host Oprah Winfrey that she never read articles that were written about her; instead she just glanced at the pictures to be sure she looked good. Her sisters teased Serena about the time she spent looking in the mirror, and, in fact, Serena's biography on the WTA Web site once listed her favorite place to visit as the mirror in her house. When she was a child, Serena starred in plays her sister Lyndrea wrote. Venus explained that Serena always had to be the princess, whereas Lyndrea was the wizard. Sister Isha described Serena by saying she was the most spoiled of all the sisters. She explained, "All of us spoil Serena, including Serena, if it's possible" (Harpo, 2002).

Serena, who made it a ritual to do her nails before a game, also believed that she must look good in order to play good tennis. She explained to Oprah, "I'm a firm believer, if you don't look good, you won't play well. And if you look bad, and your hair's messed up, or your clothes [are] wrinkled, if you don't look good, you don't play well. And that's why we play very well" (Harpo, 2002). Serena has been known for her fashion on and off the court, and she designed many of the styles she wore to play tennis.

Other Events in 1981

Iran released 52 U.S. hostages minutes after Ronald Reagan was sworn in as president of the United States.

The first recognized cases of AIDS were documented in California by the Centers for Disease Control and Prevention.

Lady Diana Spencer married Charles, Prince of Wales.

Egyptian President Anwar Sadat was assassinated.

The first U.S. test-tube baby was born.

Sandra Day O'Connor was appointed the first woman U.S. Supreme Court justice.

Pac Man was introduced in the United States.

IBM released its first personal computer.

Grandmaster Flash released the first recording using scratching in "Adventures on the Wheels of Steel."

The musical *Cats* began its run on Broadway.

MTV debuted.

Also born in 1981: Elijah Wood, Anna Kournikova, Anastasia Myskina, Roger Federer, Beyoncé Knowles, Elena Dementieva, Jenna and Barbara Bush, Britney Spears.

Indeed, her outfits on and off the court have generated much discussion, from the braided hair and beads she wore as a youth to the black, skin-tight Puma catsuit she sported at the U.S. Open in 2002 and her more recent "rebel without a cause" look. After winning her second round at the U.S. Open in 2004, Serena explained to a reporter, "I always considered myself as an entertainer. I remember always thinking of myself as a broader picture as opposed to just your normal athlete. I don't think I've ever been your normal athlete. I've always had something different going on in my life" (ASAP Sports, Serena Williams, September 1, 2004). In response to a question about the controversy her clothing choices evoked, Serena replied, "I just think I represent all females out there who believe in themselves. It doesn't matter what you look like, it's all about having confidence in you. That's not necessarily having to wear some short shorts or extremely small top, it's just about believing in yourself. I think, like, I represent that woman that believes in herself and has confidence in herself and to be unique" (ASAP Sports, Serena Williams, September 1, 2004).

As the youngest sister, Serena always faced comparisons to her older sisters, particularly Venus. Although Venus is three inches taller than Serena, Serena more than made up for this difference in height with her powerful build. When Venus told a reporter that Serena did not go to the gym to work out, that her muscular build was genetic, Serena joked: "I'm in the gym every day. I'm about to go to the gym right now, as a matter of fact (laughter). That's a joke. No, when I was born, I was 'little baby muscles.' That's just the way I came. I do go to the gym. Actually I go to the gym a little more than Venus. When I go home, I might go a little more. I've always been this way, but just to keep myself toned, I'll go to the gym. I don't want to get any bigger because it will be very unattractive. Right now it's perfect" (ASAP Sports, Serena Williams, August 31, 2000). Of course her athletic build and talent contributed enormously to her success on the tennis court.

Serena began to play tennis when she was five and a half years old. She entered 49 tournaments by age 10, winning 46 of them. When the Williams family moved to Florida in 1991, Serena went with Venus on a full scholarship to Rick Macci's prestigious tennis academy in Delray Beach, Florida. Macci, whose tennis philosophy revolves around building a relationship between coach, player, and family, also coached tennis stars Jennifer Capriati and Mary Pierce. Macci worked with Serena and Venus for four years before Richard pulled them out of the academy to work with them solely at his West Palm Beach estate. Serena stopped going to junior tennis tournaments at age 10 because her father did not want her or Venus to face racism, and he also did not want them to encounter injury or burn out like other young tennis stars. Richard witnessed the tremendous pressure many young players experienced in the junior circuit, and although critics, including Rick Macci, disapproved of him for taking Venus and Serena out of play, others, like Zina Garrison, felt that Richard should do what he thought was right for his daughters (Sparling, 2000). Richard also wanted to be sure Venus and Serena had time to focus on their education and lives outside of tennis. Under Macci's tutelage, the girls played tennis six hours a day, six days a week. They played less when Richard was in charge.

Serena turned professional in 1995 at age 14. At her first pro event, the Bell Challenge in Quebec, she was unseeded and went largely unnoticed. She lost in less than an hour of play. The next year Serena did not play any tournaments. Then, after failing to qualify for several tournaments in early 1997, she went on to participate in a tournament in Russia. She was defeated early in the tournament but went on to play in the Ameritech Cup in Chicago where she was ranked 304th by the WTA. In Chicago, she had some surprising upsets when she defeated Mary Pierce and Monica Seles before falling in the semifinal against Lindsay Davenport. She was the lowest-ranked player ever to defeat two top 10 players in the same tournament. After the Chicago victories, Serena rose quickly through the ranks of the women's tennis organization, finishing her first full season ranked 99th. By 2001, she earned the WTA number 1 singles ranking, a title she held for 57 weeks. Only Steffi Graf, Martina Navratilova, Chris Evert, Martina Hingis, and Monica Seles have held this ranking longer. Interestingly enough, Serena attributed some of the credit for her rise in the rankings to a fall from a skateboard in December 1997 (Jervis, 2002). When she fell, she landed on her left wrist, and then later that same day as she practiced on a clay court in the rain, she fell again on the same wrist. The injury and subsequent pain forced her to work on her weakest stroke, the forehand, because she could no longer play comfortably with her best stroke, the two-handed backhand. This seemed to be just what she needed. Her new, more powerful forehand greatly improved her game, and she was on her way to becoming a tennis superstar.

Serena claimed her most memorable experience was winning Wimbledon in 2002, which followed a victory at the French Open and preceded her wins at the 2002 U.S. Open and 2003 Australia Open. Her victory in Australia completed the so-called Serena Slam as she won four consecutive Grand Slam tournaments in one year's time, three in the same calendar year (2002). Only five other women, including Margaret Court, Maureen Connolly, Steffi Graf, and Monica Seles, had won three Grand

Slams in the same year. To win each of these tournaments, Serena faced and defeated Venus in the finals. Although she did not play the Australian Open in 2002, Serena returned in 2003 to win the event, defeating Venus in three sets (7–6, 3–6, 6–4). She was no longer overshadowed by her older sister Venus, no longer tagging along or trying to be just like Venus, and she was clearly getting attention on her own terms.

FREE TIME

One hobby Serena enjoyed in her free time was reading. Maya Angelou, a noted author, poet, and historian, is Serena's favorite. Angelou wrote *I Know Why the Caged Bird Sings,* an autobiography reflecting on her own life growing up as an African American in the segregated rural South. Angelou also authored other notable books, poems, and plays. Perhaps reading these stories of Angelou's experiences helped Serena to appreciate her own father's background in the rural South, a history that overlapped in many ways with Angelou's, influencing both the contexts and experiences in Serena's own life.

In addition to reading fiction and nonfiction books, Serena often worked on books that would improve her vocabulary. Serena explained: "Most of all, I remember the head teacher [at Driftwood Academy], Sandra MacManus. She had a wonderful vocabulary and it really inspired me for life, so I try to use—I'm reading a book now that's called [*Word Smart*, 3rd edition]. It's a book with vocabulary words from A to Z. I get three a day" (ASAP Sports, Serena Williams, August 31, 2001).

One of Serena's favorite pastimes was shopping. She loved to shop in major cities around the world, especially on Fifth Avenue in New York City. For shoes, she rated Bergdorf Goodman in New York City as her favorite place. She also liked to shop for shoes at Manolo Blahnik in New York City. These famous shoes by the trendy designer might retail for several thousand dollars a pair. For clothes, Serena preferred Henri Bendel and Saks in New York City. Serena also liked to shop in Soho, where she claimed there were "less expensive, fashion forward clothes" (www.serenawilliams.com). When Serena was shopping on the West Coast, she enjoyed Barney's in Los Angeles and Fred Segal.

In her free time, Serena enjoyed watching old Marilyn Monroe films, the *Lord of the Rings* trilogy, and *The Sound of Music.* Serena also liked to listen to a variety of music, including Mariah Carey and Brandy. In fact, she had a long-standing friendship with Brandy, and they were often seen together at public events and awards ceremonies. They attended Los Angeles Clippers basketball games, the ESPY Awards, and other high-profile events. Brandy also was spotted at tennis matches to cheer on her famous sister friends. At the 2001 U.S. Open, she held a sign that read, "It's Venus's planet. We just live here." Brandy was there to cheer both sisters later in the same tournament when they faced each other in the historic finals.

Outside of these leisure activities, Serena participated in a number of clinics to help teach urban youth how to play tennis, and she made numerous appearances at schools and for charitable and community organizations, particularly those that target programs for at-risk youth. There is a Venus and Serena Williams Tutorial/Tennis Academy in Los Angeles to provide inner-city kids with academic and tennis resources that would allow them to attend the college of their choice (see http://www.venus serenatennisacademy.org). The academy included after-school programs, summer camps, mentorship programs, and more.

In addition to her involvement with her mother's OWL Foundation, Serena was involved in a variety of philanthropic work, including serving as an advocate for ovarian cancer research and the homeless. She was also a spokesperson for the American Library Association's Celebrity READ campaign. This campaign conveyed a simple message, "read," through posters and bookmarks that showed celebrities with books. Serena's poster and bookmark contain a picture of her standing behind a tennis net holding a copy of *A Raisin in the Sun*, the award-winning 1959 play by Lorraine Hansberry about a poor African American family in Chicago that struggles to overcome poverty and harsh living conditions.

LOOK AT ME!

When she was 20 years old, Serena began to dabble in professional acting. Her first experience was in 2001 when she made a guest appearance with Venus as a voice on the animated television show *The Simpsons*. She signed with the William Morris Agency and began to do more television roles than film because of the time commitment involved in film roles. Television seemed to be easier to fit around her tennis schedule.

In 2001, Serena made a cameo appearance in Martin Lawrence's movie *Black Knight*. After this, Serena appeared as a schoolteacher in *My Wife and Kids*, starring Damon Wayans, on ABC in October 2002. On October 22, 2003, Serena appeared in a dramatic role on a Showtime episode of *Street Time*. Then during summer 2003, Serena filmed a part for the movie *Beauty Shop*, starring Queen Latifah (a spin-off of the box-office hit *Barbershop*, starring Ice Cube).

Some critics wondered if her tennis playing would suffer due to her acting schedule. Although Serena felt that balancing acting and tennis was something she would have to do, she also noted that, "It's a totally different world and far more glamorous than tennis but I love tennis because it's a big part of my life" (Guardian, 2004). Yet, it was not easy to convince her fans that she was balancing these two interests very well. In summer 2003, she was supposed to play the Rogers AT&T Cup in Toronto, and much media hype surrounded the elite players who would compete in this event. Canadians expected that their ticket purchases would allow them to see Serena in action, unless she had some unforeseen injury. Then Serena withdrew from the tournament on July 18, 2003, just weeks before the event, citing a scheduling conflict. As it turns out, Street Time was shooting in Toronto at the same time (see Toombs, 2003). When a reporter later questioned her interest in acting, Serena explained, "Well, I've had a lot of opportunities. A lot of people say that, you know, 'Serena isn't serious about her tennis, she wants to go to Hollywood,' which is true. I would love to get a lot of acting gigs. But you wouldn't believe the stuff I turn down because of my tournament schedule. I'm like, 'Okay, I can't do that. I'm trying to play tennis here.'" (ASAP Sports, Serena Williams, March 26, 2004). Time will tell where Serena's true passions and interests lie, but for now, it seems that she is committed to tennis first, at least in word (but perhaps not in deed).

LIFE AT THE MANSION

In 2000, Serena and Venus purchased a $2.7 million mansion in Palm Beach, Florida, just 15 minutes from the Williams family's estate. Venus and Serena live together at their new mansion with their dogs. Venus's terrier, Bob, keeps company with Serena's two dogs, a Parson Russell terrier named Jackie and a pit bull named Bambi. Serena bought the pit bull after moving into the mansion with Venus. They were home alone quite a bit, and Serena felt they needed to have a bigger dog around (Harpo, 2002). Serena often referred to the dogs as her sons, and both Venus and Serena had the dogs accompany them on their travels and shopping excursions whenever it was possible. Once they were "tag-team" shopping in a Saks Fifth Avenue store in Charleston, South Carolina, and store manager, Lori Saad, noted the flying camisoles, the chaos of the dressing room, and the teeny dog with them who "just sat on the couch and watched" (Tresniowski & Rozsa, 2004, p. 138).

When talking about their life together, the sisters joked about various responsibilities they shared (or not). Perhaps the biggest difference involved food and cooking. Serena explained, "I eat to live, I don't live to eat. So I eat the minimal amount of food that I can so I can stay in shape. Venus always gets angry at me because I never go grocery shopping, I never buy food. She always tells me to go to the store, and I never go. It's good. She always cooks, but she's very upset at me all the time, 'Serena, you never go to the store.' I'm like, 'Yeah, you know.' I'm very lazy about that. When we stay at home, there's nothing in our refrigerator. Some people came over one time, our friends, they were like, 'You have nothing in your refrigerator.' There was nothing to eat. Our cereal has bugs in it because it's so old. My mom sometimes brings things over. Sometimes she goes to the grocery store and cooks for us." Then she joked, "Life is so tough" (ASAP Sports, Serena Williams, June 24, 2002). Serena liked to eat out at a variety of restaurants, including Mr. Chow, PF Chang's, McDonald's, and Roscoe Chicken and Waffles.

In 2002, Serena purchased a $1.4 million condominium in Westside, California. According to *Forbes* magazine, the condo is 2,000 square feet with two bedrooms, valet parking, a fitness center and a pool, a concierge, and security. In part, this pointed to her newfound independence from Venus. She was striking out on her own, symbolically and practically, to the degree that she would be closer to acting possibilities in Los Angeles. She was finding her own way. As Venus explained, "Serena knows exactly what she wants in life. And if she doesn't know, then I help her to know. She definitely has her mind made up on things. She loves to be confused because of the luxury of being confused. She likes to be out of control because it's fun to be out of control. She likes to amuse herself by playing games and telling jokes. And sometimes she even gets mad at me on the doubles court" (Aronson, 2001, pp. 49–50).

Serena has been linked romantically during the past several years to a few famous boyfriends. In 2003, she was connected to Dallas Cowboys' wide receiver Keyshawn Johnson, a rumor they both publicly denied after they were seen together at Mr. Chow in Los Angeles and other clubs. It also was widely rumored that Brandy arranged for Serena to meet Los Angeles Clippers basketball player Corey Maggette. However, Serena has protected this private part of her life from the press as much as possible. Serena told *Ebony* in 2002 that she looks for intelligence in her boyfriends. She explained, "I think what's really attractive is a man who can think for himself, has his own mind, and has a lot of self-confidence. I'm not shallow. If you're dumb, I can't really talk to you. A lot of people don't have any confidence. And when they get around me, they won't believe I like them and not anybody else. And before you know it, I'm solo again" (Chappell, 2002, p.164).

In 2004 Serena began the most public and controversial of her relationships when she began dating Hollywood director Brett Ratner, who directed the action comedy *Rush Hour*. They were seen together at the French Open and the Cannes Film Festival, and they were spotted at various events around Hollywood, Palm Beach, and London. Ratner also sat with the Williams family at the 2004 U.S. Open. This relationship stirred a bit of controversy among some of Serena's fans because Ratner was white, and many wondered how Richard Williams was handling this out of the public eye. Those who knew him well realized that he was not keen on interracial relationships. At one point, several years before Serena and Ratner were dating, the message Richard recorded on his answering machine said, "There are those that ask me what I think of intermarriage. Anyone that's marrying outside of the race that's black should be hung by their necks at sundown. Please leave a message" (Wertheim, 2002, p. 75). Perhaps he had a change of heart when Serena introduced him to Ratner; perhaps he did not. But at the U.S. Open, all seemed to be well, and Richard even loaned his camera to the famous film director.

"I'M GLAD I DIDN'T SHRINK"

As she grew older, Serena continued to be inspired by her sister Venus, even though she no longer felt she needed to be just like her "For me, it served as a great inspiration because we both grew up together practicing on the same courts, the same thing, every day working really hard. Obviously when she was doing very well, I wanted to be there. I saw everything she was having, getting. I wanted it also. I wanted to be up top. I wanted to be a player. I wanted to be a Grand Slam champion. I wanted to be the best. That's what I'm still trying to work for. I'm glad I didn't shrink" (ASAP Sports, June 27, 2001). It could hardly be said that Serena shrank from anything. As she grew away from her need to be Venus and came into her own, she made her mark, continuing to strive to be the best. It is difficult to predict what her lasting legacy to tennis or acting will be because it seems she has only just begun.

In 1998 an 18-year old Venus shows her strength, power and concentration as she returns a ball to a competitor. *Courtesy: Photofest.*

A glamorous Venus anticipates a serve during a match in 2000. *Courtesy: Photofest.*

Serena appears on court at the U.S. Open in 2001 in Flushing Meadows, New York. *Courtesy: Photofest.*

Venus and Serena often make public appearances together as they receive awards for their accomplishments. In this photo, they are being honored at the 15th Annual Essence Awards at Madison Square Garden (May 24, 2001). *Courtesy: Photofest.*

Serena enjoys making television appearances—both as an actor and a guest on talk shows. She appeared on *Jimmy Kimmel Live*, an ABC late night talk show on November 7, 2003. *Courtesy: Photofest.*

Serena and Venus Williams appear at news conference to launch their new book *How to Play Tennis* at the Wimbledon Tennis Club (June 17, 2004.) © Topham/The Image Works.

Chapter 5

TENNIS

Although Venus and Serena were the first African American sisters to face one another across the court in a professional tennis match, they were not the first sisters to compete against one another in a championship match. Sisters Maud and Lilian Watson, ages 19 and 26, respectively, competed against each other in the first ladies' lawn tennis championship at the All England Croquet and Lawn Tennis Club in Wimbledon, England, in 1884. The younger sister, Maud, took first place, and Lilian took second. Then Anne and Elizabeth Minter met in the finals of the U.S. Open in 1985, followed by Manuela and Katerina Maleeva, who met in the U.S. Open in 1990 and the Australian Open in 1991. Although Venus and Serena were not the first sisters to square off against one another in a tennis match, they were certainly the sister act that would compete in more Grand Slam and tournament finals, and they were by far the most famous and controversial.

Serena and Venus first faced each other in a women's tennis championship final on March 28, 1999, at the Lipton Championships in Key Biscayne, Florida. Venus and Serena played intensely against one another, but unlike the Watson sisters, this time the older sister would win first place and the younger second. As they competed, their father, Richard, watched from the stands, writing messages with a grease pencil on a white board, the first of which was "Welcome to the Williams Show!" His long-standing predictions about his daughters' domination in the sport seemed to be coming true. In 1999, the girls were on the brink of tennis history, and they would soon find themselves with Grand Slam titles, gold medals, and the number 1 and number 2 WTA rankings. They certainly had come a long way from the ghetto.

THE BEGINNINGS

In 1984, Richard Williams loaded his four-and-a-half-year-old daughter Venus in his Volkswagen van and drove her to the public tennis courts on the corner of East Compton and Atlantic Boulevards in Compton, California. He had been collecting tennis balls and finally had about 500 that he stored in an old shopping cart in the back of his van. When father and daughter arrived at the cracked asphalt courts, sparkling from the sun reflecting off the broken glass, he began to toss the balls to his daughter, one at a time, and she hit them back to him. When he finished, Venus cried, and so he continued to toss a few more balls to her before they went home. She loved to play tennis from the first time she held a racquet in her hand. The difficulty Richard experienced getting her to stop playing would be a pattern in the years to come.

A year after Venus began to play tennis, Serena joined her father and sister in their daily treks to the court. As the trio became regulars, they grew acquainted with other people at the park, including future rap stars Easy-E and Snoop Doggy Dogg. Yet, the courts were in a dangerous part of town. Gunfire was the norm in Compton's poverty-stricken and crime-ridden neighborhood, and it often could be heard near the park where the girls played. It certainly was not always a safe place for them to be. One day as the girls practiced, a gang lieutenant sprayed gunfire over the tennis court as he stood up through the sunroof of his car. Needless to say, Oracene was not pleased when the girls returned home and reported how they dove for cover as the bullets showered around them. She knew they lived in a dangerous neighborhood and that the threat of violence was all around them. Yet, she and Richard decided they should continue to live in the ghetto. After all, this was their neighborhood. They moved to Compton in 1983 when Venus and Serena were just babies, and they were committed to the community, at least for the time being.

As young girls, Venus and Serena continued to play tennis each day, and they grew to understand the game. They watched tapes and television clips of tennis players. The sisters especially liked to watch John McEnroe because they admired his aggressive playing style (Aronson, 2001). By the time the girls were old enough to watch McEnroe play, he had made tremendous accomplishments in the world of tennis. He was the number 1 ranked player in the world between 1981 and 1984, a four-time U.S. Open champion, a three-time winner at Wimbledon, and the winner of five Davis Cups. Although he had tremendous talent on the tennis court and was known for his serve-and-volley style of play, he also had a temper that earned him the nick-name "Superbrat." He often yelled at tournament officials if he disagreed with a call, and he threw tantrums and pouted on the court. The girls did not learn this aspect of his game from viewing the tapes. As they grew older, they were known for their composure on the court. Rarely, if ever, did they dispute a call, even if it was clearly an error by a tournament official.

Richard was eager to see his daughters become tennis champions, and he told neighbors and friends from the time the girls were young that they eventually would become number 1 and number 2 in the world. Despite the unlikely nature of these claims, he remained committed to their po-tential for success. At the same time, he seemed to temper his ambitious goals for his daughters with a practice schedule that was less rigorous than many of the girls' peers in the sport. Venus and Serena practiced just two and a half hours, three days each week, whereas many of their peers prac-ticed longer hours for five or six days each week. Practice for the girls in-cluded much encouragement and support, hugs and kisses, and fun. Even as the girls grew older and found success in the game, Richard would be sure they took breaks and went on vacations, often scheduling them the week before a major tournament. In fall 1998, when Venus was ranked 5th and Serena was ranked 20th in the world, Richard told the press, "My girls are very great players, and they'll win lots of tournaments, but I'll tell you what I tell them: Education is much more important" (Aronson, 2001, p. 40). Indeed if they had homework or if their grades slipped even just a bit, Richard would not let them play tennis. He recognized that tennis careers could be short-lived: an injury, burnout, or any other factor could interfere with their play. He believed they needed to excel academi-cally if they were to meet with success in life.

By the time Venus was 10 years old, Richard was not telling only friends and family about his daughters' future. He announced to the press that his daughters would be the top-ranked tennis players in the world. By the time Venus was 11 years old, she already had gained much attention for her playing ability and for the potential people saw in her. She was win-ning junior tournaments, and major endorsements were imminent. As people became increasingly impressed with Venus, Richard told them to watch out for Serena as well. He felt she would be an even better player than her older sister. But as youngsters, it seemed that Serena was destined to be just a few steps behind her older sister.

THE JUNIOR CIRCUIT

When they were living in southern California, Venus and Serena excelled on the junior circuit. At age 10, Venus was serving the ball at record-breaking speed, nearly 100 miles per hour. By the time she was 12, Venus had a 63–0 record on the USTA junior tour. Serena was not too far behind her older sister. By 10, she already had won 46 of the 49 matches she had played.

As young players, Venus and Serena were influenced by many tennis professionals of the time in different ways. In 1988, John McEnroe and Pete Sampras hit tennis balls with Venus after watching her work out with teaching professional Paul Cohen in Brentwood, California. Although Richard Williams told Venus that McEnroe took it easy on her, she did not believe him and instead told her father that she could have beaten McEnroe. As a player on the junior circuit, Venus admired Gabriela Sabatini, the Argentinean player who defeated Steffi Graf to win the 1990 U.S. Open. Sabatini was known for her backhand and for her beauty, and she was the first tennis player to have a doll made in her image by the Great American Doll Company. As a young and aspiring tennis player, Venus probably never imagined that she, too, would one day have a doll made in her image.

As a junior player, Venus also admired Boris Becker's play, and she tried to serve like him. Becker, a German player who in 1985 as a 17-year-old became the youngest male player to win Wimbledon, was known for his powerful and often unreturnable serves. Venus also looked up to Monica Seles, the Yugoslav-born U.S. tennis player who won the French Open at age 16 in 1990. Venus claimed that when she was about 10 years old, she began to grunt like Monica when she played tennis (ASAP Sports, Venus Williams, August 26, 2001).

After Venus and Serena began winning more junior tournaments in the early 1990s, Richard and Oracene began to worry that the girls' fame would make it even more difficult for the family to live in Compton. The girls were earning trophies and prizes, and some corporations were beginning to pursue them for major endorsement deals. People knew where they lived and expected that they had money as a result of the girls' accomplishments. Due to these concerns, in 1991 Richard sold his security business and moved the family to Florida, where the girls were awarded full scholarships to attend the Haines City tennis academy. At the academy, Rick Macci became their coach. The girls were on their way to making their father's predictions come true. When the Williams sisters left southern California, Venus was ranked 1st in the 12 and under division and Serena was number 1 in the 10 and under division of the state's junior circuit. The girls had experienced much success on this tour, endorsement deals were sure to come, and they had much to look forward to in Florida.

After they were settled in their new home and school, however, Rich-ard decided to pull the girls off the junior circuit. Although many advised him against this, including coach Rick Macci, Richard thought this move would lower the possibility of injury or burnout. Oracene agreed with his decision. As she explained, "There's so much pressure. Most kids don't want to disappoint their parents. I see a lot of talented kids, but they don't look happy. It's none of my business, but I think they would be happier if they did other things, too" (Michie, 2003).

Some felt the decision to take the girls off the junior tour certainly would ruin their chances of playing professional tennis. A tennis tourna-ment was a difficult place, and without the practice and socializing that came on the junior tour, critics felt the girls never would be able to with-stand the pressure and competition on the professional tour. Looking back on this decision, it is difficult to know whether playing the junior tour-naments would have helped the girls or not. They certainly met much success without it. In fact, in 2000 when Serena was asked by a reporter whether playing the junior circuit would have made a difference for her or not in relation to her tennis career, she stood by her father's decision. Serena explained, "Everyone has a different heart. Everyone has a differ-ent body. Everyone does different things. I think for Venus and I, we just tried a different road, and it worked for us. I can't tell you whether if I would have played junior tennis or not, it would have been different one way or the other because I didn't play, so I really am not able to distin-guish whether it would have been. But I think at some point I might have been slightly jaded due to the fact that I would have traveled to France, I would have been to Australia, I would have been to England, I would have been here. By the time I come to the professionals myself, I get bored easily, I would have been slightly jaded" (ASAP Sports, Serena Williams, September 2, 2000).

Shortly after deciding to pull the girls off the junior tour, Richard made a second controversial decision. In 1995, he took the girls out of Macci's tennis academy, only four years after they began their training with the famous coach. Rather than have the girls attend the academy and re-ceive professional coaching through the school's staff, Richard and Ora-cene would coach their daughters at their home, orchestrating a variety of hitting coaches, trainers, and advisory coaches, and they would manage Venus's and Serena's careers on their own. This decision remains con-tentious to this day. On September 29, 2004, the *New York Daily News* reported that Macci was planning to write a tell-all book about his four years coaching the Williams sisters. Richard Williams planned to sue Macci if he followed through with the book, stating that it was a publicity stunt and breach of contract; yet, Macci claimed that it was Williams who broke the contract by minimizing his role in the sisters' success and by publicly defaming him. There certainly seemed to be no shortage of storm surrounding this family and their coaching decisions.

TENNIS TRAINING THE WILLIAMS WAY

Tennis training at the Williams's estate in Florida was uniquely a family affair. The tennis courts were not far from the white two-story mansion where the family lived, and the girls made their way to the courts each day with their dogs in tow, often tumbling or doing cartwheels along the way. Richard typically maneuvered around the courts and the estate in a white golf cart, overseeing the affairs of the girls' practice. Even if he was not always physically present, there were prompts from him everywhere the girls looked. Around the courts, Richard posted handmade signs to remind the sisters to work on specific aspects of their game. The signs, which looked like "for sale" signs that people post in their yards, sometimes related to psychological aspects of the game as much as they did to specific tennis skills. Printed in large, clear block letters, the signs read "VENUS YOU MUST TAKE CONTROL OF YOUR FUTURE" and "SERENA YOU MUST LEARN TO USE MORE TOP SPIN ON THE BALL" (Jervis, 2002). Both girls kept note cards courtside with similar reminders, such as "Bend your knees," when they played tournaments, and they read and paid attention to these reminders as a way to keep their game focused.

Typical training days and practice sessions for the girls began with warm-ups, which might include five minutes of aerobic exercise, followed by stretches. Then the girls would spend a few hours working on various drills and practices on the court. One of Venus's former hitting coaches, Dave Rineberg, played tennis against the girls on a daily basis to help improve their game. One practice technique Rineberg used involved using strategies and skills that simulated the typical game of many of the pro tennis players at the time. In other words, he would pretend to be Steffi Graf, Arantxa Sanchez-Vicario, or Martina Navratilova, among others, and he would play against Venus or Serena imitating shots and game strategies typical of these players. This would help the sisters to think through their strategies and shots as they worked to improve their game (Rineberg, 2003).

In addition to hitting practice on the court, Venus and Serena worked through various drills that were intended to help specific aspects of their game. For example, when Venus needed to improve her wrist pronation so that she could have more power in her serve, Rineberg had Venus take her old, broken tennis racquets and throw them high in the air using a service motion. This helped her to have a better wrist snap, which in turn improved her serve (Rineberg, 2003).

After their practice sessions ended, Venus and Serena often did fitness training. This would involve anything from running to biking and working their arms, legs, and core. Kerrie Brooks joined the sisters as a trainer in 2000, around the time of the French Open, and she seemed to be a welcome addition to the Williams team. Venus did not like going to the gym to work out, so having a trainer was important to her. She explained, "I don't like the gym. I don't think I ever will. So it's important that I would have a trainer, or else I will not work hard in the gym. I'll work hard on the tennis court" (ASAP Sports, Venus Williams, June 26, 2000).

Although Venus and Serena have had hitting partners, trainers, and advisory coaches, such as Morris King Jr., over the years, their parents ultimately have made the decisions about their coaching and training schedules. Many have questioned this choice, including former tennis champion Tracy Austin. During the 2004 U.S. Open, Austin suggested that Venus, who committed 42 unforced errors before falling to Lindsay Davenport in a quarterfinal match, would benefit from professional coaching for her troubled forehand shot, which had become quite inconsistent. Twenty of these unforced errors were on the forehand, but 18 winners were likewise with a forehand shot. In spite of this and many similar criticisms they received across the years for coaching Venus and Serena on their own, Richard and Oracene vehemently defended their decision to continue to coach their daughters. In fact, Richard became quite defensive in response to Tracy Austin's comment, publicly stating, "I can't care what Tracy or anyone says. When Venus and Serena were winning, there wasn't something wrong. Now they're losing, there's something wrong. I think it's a disgrace how the system [works] against those two black girls. It would be interesting to look at Tracy's family background—her family life must have been terrible" (Austin, 2004). Tracy Austin and other sports writers felt it was a shame that Richard turned her analysis of Venus's game into a personal attack that raised questions of racism. Austin later noted that Venus was "much too talented to be ranked No. 12 in the world" (Austin, 2004). Most tennis players train with former professionals across their careers, and the suggestion was not so much a critique of Venus's coaching as it was a suggestion to help improve her tennis. Austin had taken a similar strategy in her own professional tennis career, selecting coaches who would help her to work on different aspects of her game. She worked with Robert Lansdorp from her childhood throughout her career, and later with Marty Rieseen and Roy Emerson. She credited each coach with adding to her game in different ways. Much like the Williams family's decision to take the girls from the junior tour, however, the decision to keep Richard Williams as their primary coach would leave only questions of what might have been had they trained differently.

Richard's behavior at tournaments was considered to be quite odd and unpredictable by many observers. He was seen dancing in the stands, holding white boards with messages that seemed to be directed more to the press and viewing audience than to his daughters, and he often left tournaments unexpectedly. At the 2001 U.S. Open, author L. Jon Wertheim noted that Richard spent much of the tournament in the photographers' pit shooting countless rolls of film, many while the lens cap was still on the camera. When he was not doing this, he was talking about writing a cartoon book or doing missionary work in Australia. Then, before Venus and Serena met in the finals, he took a plane to Florida, declaring that his work at the tournament was finished. Although it was widely reported at the time that his marriage to Oracene had dissolved, he did not sit in the stands to observe the girls' game as most coaches did. Instead, he went quietly away. Perhaps he felt his presence at the tournament would distract from the girls' accomplishments, or perhaps he had other deals to make or business to attend to (in 1999, he claimed that he began three new businesses each year). With Richard Williams, it was difficult to guess.

In spite of the controversy surrounding their father and the general perception that he was very controlling, both girls seemed to admire him and to be thankful for his influence. Venus explained, "He knows the best for me. I think he knows the game better than any one else. And I enjoy working with him because he always has a new idea ... a new innovation.... That's what I like the most about working with him" (Jervis, 2002). Venus explained at a press conference at the 1998 U.S. Open about her father, "He's real funny. He doesn't put any pressure on us. He said, 'Venus, don't you think you're playing too many tournaments. How long you going to be overseas?' So I say, 'It's not that many, Dad.' He doesn't like it that I stay away from home too much. I'm not sure how much I like it either. But I think that there's only so many years that I'll have, so I should take advantage. And I think he looks out for us a lot also. He wants the best for us. And he takes care of the dogs also. They really like him. They might like him more than us because he buys hams and hot dogs for them, and I won't do it. He lets them ride in the car also, and I don't do that too often because I don't want to clean, so" (ASAP Sports, Venus Williams, September 7, 1998).

Serena likewise spoke of her admiration for her father as he balanced being a father, a coach, and a manager. She said, "As a manager, I think he's the best. He has produced Venus and Serena Williams. So what better can you do. I just don't think, I can't think of much better someone could do. Not just one champion, but two" (Jervis, 2002).

Oracene Price, who often was overshadowed in public by Richard but nevertheless remained a strong force in her daughters' careers, offered a different courtside presence than Richard. While he worked on the particulars of his daughters' tennis games, Oracene seemed to work on their psychological and emotional well-being. Serena described her mother's coaching when she explained, "My mom, if you take a human being, you have a body, she would be the spine, where you can't move without it, you can't do anything. I would say that's her. She was there in the beginning of our career, and she really supported us the way your spine would, help you stand straight. She was there the whole time. She really—I called her and said. I said, 'Mom, what do I need to do?' just before my match. Apparently she gave me some good advice. My dad is here. He's helping us practicing. I'm like, 'Mom, what do you think?' She's our coach. That's why she travels with us" (ASAP Sports, Serena Williams, March 14, 2001).

The Williams sisters' relationship with their parents as coaches seemed to be much more harmonious, at least on the surface, than other parent/coach–child/player relationships on the tennis circuit. Martina Hingis and her mother, Melanie Molitor, a former professional tennis player, experienced a tumultuous relationship as Molitor attempted to coach her daughter in tennis. In 2001, Hingis broke from her mother, declaring that she needed a change, but then the two reunited six weeks later, in time for Hingis to fail to make it out of the first round at Wimbledon. The relationship between tennis fathers and daughters has had a long history of being notoriously turbulent. Jim Pierce, Mary Pierce's father, was reported to have physically abused his daughter, and he was known for berating her in public. Steffi Graf's father kept her isolated from the other women on the tour, and he was known to embarrass her publicly. Stefano Capriati, Jennifer's father, once bragged about making her do sit-ups in her crib. He explained that he pushed her into professional tennis at age 13 because she might burn out, and if she did, at least she would have more money than he would be able to give to her. And Damir Dokic, Jelena Dokic's father, was known for his abusiveness and public drunkenness, which sometimes resulted in him being banned from tournament venues (for further details on each of these instances, see Wertheim, 2002).

There are various reasons why parents tend to be so involved with tennis when their children are players. Wertheim (2002) noted that the developmental timeline for players is one factor. Like Venus and Serena, players who go on to professional tennis typically hit hundreds of tennis balls each day before they are tall enough to see over the net. There has not been a successful professional tennis player who began to play as a teenager. Typically, the parents must make such a choice for the child, and along with this choice, both parents and children must make many sacrifices. In addition to the developmental timeline, Wertheim observed that tennis is not a particularly complicated sport. It consists of a half-dozen basic strokes, and even fathers like Richard Williams who have no basic training in tennis are able to catch on to the game well enough to feel they can provide coaching for their child. Of course, whether they actually can provide this coaching as well as they imagine is difficult to say. Parents are much less likely to take on coaching situations if a child is talented in other arenas: music, art, dance, or even golfing.

The Williams family remained unique compared to these other families who seemed to struggle with relationships that involved coaching. There seemed to be cohesion and agreement within the family about the coaching arrangement Richard and Oracene established, and never once did the girls publicly doubt or question their parents' abilities or intent with their careers. At the 2000 Wimbledon tournament, Venus explained how her parents balance these responsibilities. She said, "My dad does most of the stuff at home. They usually take turns on the Tours. Some tournaments like the Lipton or Indian Wells or U.S. Open are together. But usually they take shifts. For a coach, if it's your job, if that's where you make your earning, living, it's what you do, what you like, but when you're the parent, sure you want to be the coach, but you also have your own life. That's why it's great that they can take turns" (ASAP Sports, Venus Williams, June 28, 2000). In spite of Richard and Oracene's obvious eccentricities (Richard's behavior and Oracene's sometimes unusual choices in hair color and clothing), Venus and Serena seemed to be content with their tennis training.

THE PROFESSIONAL TENNIS CIRCUIT

The WTA tennis tour had changed dramatically in the years before Venus and Serena entered professional tennis. What once had been an "oatmeal-bland collection of moonballing baseliners struggling for fans and respect," had turned into a "Generation Next, equal parts attitude and pulchritude, raised in an era of heroine chic, in which Buff is Beautiful, and trashtalking is just keeping things real" (Wertheim, 2002, p. 3). From the days of Chris Evert and Martina Navratilova to Gabriela Sabatini and Steffi Graf, professional tennis never before had garnered attention through news media, television coverage, and marketing as it did with the era ushered in by Lindsay Davenport, Anna Kournikova, Martina Hingis, and Venus and Serena Williams. One of the moments when it was most obvious that times had changed came during the 2001 U.S. Open when Venus and Serena faced one another in the finals. This was the first time a women's final was aired during prime time. The event drew 22.7 million viewers, more than any other television event that day, and it was described as "electric" in the way a Hollywood awards show would feel (Wertheim, 2002). Celebrities, including Jay-Z, P. Diddy, Allan Houston, Joe Namath, Sarah Jessica Parker, Robert Redford, and Brandy, were in the stands as Diana Ross sang the opening rendition of *America the Beautiful*. This was certainly a new time and a new place for women's tennis, and Venus and Serena were center stage.

Of course, the road to Arthur Ashe stadium on this celebratory evening had not been an easy one for these two young athletes. In addition to the long years of practice, the Williams sisters endured much personal struggle as well. The WTA is notoriously hard on up-and-coming young stars, and Venus and Serena had not spent time on the junior tour preparing for this in the ways other players had. They did not spend time getting to know other players. By the time they turned professional, some of the women's tennis players had spent years together in the players' lounges, enduring both triumphs and tragedies together. The tour is known for being unkind to new members, but for Venus and Serena, the professional tour could be an especially cruel place. L. Jon Wertheim (2002) observed, "[The] antipathy for the Williams sisters runs deeper than any hazing ritual—one player reported that as Serena stumbled through the early rounds, 'girls who had barely met before were giving each other high fives'" (p. 19). The Williams family tended to keep to themselves in the players' lounge, bringing even more resentment as they shared jokes and laughed together. Their seeming disinterest in forging friendships with other players on the tour drew criticism from other athletes, including Lindsay Davenport, and from high-profile sports figures like John McEnroe.

The WTA tour has been a predominantly white arena, and it is certainly important to wonder whether the sisters felt ostracized on the tour because of their race. Wertheim (2002) observed that, with the exception of Wimbledon, where whiteness pervades every aspect of the tournament, from the clothing to the fans, "race is generally a nonissue on the Tour" (p. 163). Wertheim did note that although racism was an issue for Zina Garrison, who was a player on the tour just a few years before Venus and Serena, Garrison did not attribute her treatment to the tour itself. Garrison was sometimes not allowed on tournament sites because security guards did not believe she really was a tournament player, and she felt she lost out on millions in endorsement deals because she was not "right" for the contract (Wertheim, 2002, p. 165). In spite of these issues, Garrison never claimed that the tour was racist, nor that there was institutionalized racism or bigotry on the tour. Wertheim, citing African American tennis player Lori McNeil, credits the international aspects of the tour for increasing players' tolerance and respect of difference.

In time, the sisters did make friends on the tour, including two other young African American players. In 2002, Serena explained., "Chanda [Rubin] and I really get along well. Alexandra and I, Alexandra Stevenson, we're really good friends. And Kim, she's a very nice girl. We always talk. There's a lot of players—Lisa Raymond, Rennae Stubbs. We definitely get along" (ASAP Sports, Serena Williams, July 6, 2002).

In 1998, the sisters launched their own newspaper, *The Tennis Monthly Recap*, perhaps in a gesture to have a different role and impact on the tour. They began the newsletter when the girls became discouraged that the news media seemed to be reporting only negative aspects of tennis and the professional tour. Emblazoned on the front cover was the disclaimer "Please excuse all mistakes" and the proclamation of Venus and Serena as "Editor Chief" of the paper (Wertheim, 2002). Serena credited Venus with the idea, and she wrote her first story on the great Brazilian hope. Venus wrote about the Chase Championships. They distributed the first 30 copies at the Australian Open in January 1999. Subsequent issues featured stories on Pete Sampras, a tribute to Steffi Graf, stories about their dogs, and tour gossip. They wrote the articles, printed the newsletter, and distributed copies in locker rooms at big tournaments. Some on the tour felt this was bizarre, particularly because Venus and Serena seemed to steer clear of socializing with others on the tour (Wertheim, 2002), yet many players seemed to read and enjoy the articles. They continued with the newspaper until the early 2000s when their schedules no longer permitted them the extensive time they needed to work on it.

WILLIAMS VERSUS WILLIAMS

In 1998, after her rise from 304th to 99th in the WTA rankings, Serena won her way to the semifinals of the Australian Open when she defeated then number 2 ranked American Lindsay Davenport. Next she faced her sister Venus, and they made tennis history again as the first African American sisters to face off against one another in a major tournament. Venus won the semifinal match and later explained to the press, "It wasn't fun eliminating my little sister, but I have to be tough. After the match, I said 'I'm sorry I had to take you out.' Since I am older, I have the feeling

I should win. I really wouldn't want to lose. But that's the only person I would be happy losing to because I would say, 'Go ahead, Serena. Go ahead, take the title.'" Serena also commented, "If I had to lose in the second round, there's no one better to lose to than Venus" (Aronson, 2001, p. 39). Venus seemed to anticipate what would become commonplace for the two sisters over the next several years as she told the international press, "Serena hates to lose and her reputation is she doesn't lose to anyone twice, so I'm going to be practicing secretly if I want to win the next one" (Aronson, 2001, p. 40).

As Venus and Serena began to dominate the professional tennis circuit, they faced one another in matches on a more regular basis. These matches, which initially drew much hype among fans and the media, were often a source of disappointment. The sisters did not seem to play their best tennis against one another. This could be attributed to any number of reasons. For one, they knew one another's games better than anyone else did. It would be difficult for one sister to surprise the other with some new aspect of her game. Further, some wondered how the girls would fare in such high-pressure competition given their close relationship. Venus seemed to be particularly vulnerable in these situations, and indeed, when she defeated Serena in the semifinals at Wimbledon in 2000, Serena reportedly cried for half an hour in a bathroom stall in the women's locker room before facing the press (Wertheim, 2002). In the press conference after the match, Venus admitted that it was difficult for her to see her sister lose, particularly because she was the one who needed to look out for her little sister. She said, "But still I am the big sister, so I am always worried about her.... You know, she's a younger sister. You know, that's the way it is when you're younger. You always get your way. You know, anyone who's had a younger sibling knows that. When they don't get their way, mom and dad step in, 'Give her the ice cream.' As far as the older sister, you know, or the older brother, you know, you roll with the punches. If you win or you lose, you don't get the ice cream, it's okay" (ASAP Sports, Venus Williams, July 6, 2000). In time, Serena would win her share of matches against Venus, and Venus would find herself understanding Serena's feelings quite well.

Many players and fans questioned whether Richard Williams or one of the girls decided before a big match who would come out the winner. Wertheim (2002, p. 178) cites a source close to the Williams family, who claimed that Richard gave explicit instructions to his daughters that Venus should win in three sets before the girls played one another in the 1999 Key Biscayne match. Another source had a similar story, claiming that Richard told the girls that whoever won the first set should win the match in three sets, primarily because of the endorsement deals that were pending. The longer the match went, the more opportunity potential sponsors would have to observe the girls and realize their domination of the sport. Of course Richard denies that any set was ever fixed or determined in advance. Venus went on to win the Key Biscayne match in three sets, but their play against one another was awkward at best. Fans witnessed them commit a combined 107 unforced errors (Wertheim, 2002, p. 176). In spite of this and similar disappointments in their play against each other, Richard insisted that the girls always played their best when they competed in all-Williams games. He was certain they both competed to win. For those who believed otherwise, he said, "The media is trying to nullify what Venus and Serena have done, cast a shadow on the family.... I have never asked Venus or Serena to lose a match. When Serena lost at Wimbledon [last year], she cried like hell, not because someone asked her to lose, but because Serena hates to lose. Venus isn't like that. When Venus loses, she walks off the court and is ready to get something to eat" (*Jet*, April 9, 2001).

After her loss to Venus in the U.S. Open finals in 2001, Serena told reporters, "She said she didn't feel like she really won because she always wanted to, you know, kind of protect me. I told her, 'Well, you won. Take it. You know, it's your win. It's your victory. If I would have won, I won. You won, you need it. It's yours. Don't feel that way because, honestly, there's not enough time in one's life. Time happens so fast.' I just told her, you know, 'It's yours. You won it'" (ASAP Sports, Serena Williams, September 8, 2001). Venus seemed to struggle with the victory as she explained, "I just hate to see Serena lose anyway—even against me. So I think that's the harder part. For anything, it would be easier for her to beat me, then I'd maybe be, I don't know, happier. It's kind of strange. But when you're the big sister looking to take care of the younger one.... If I was playing a different opponent, I'd probably be a lot more joyful. But I'm happy I won the U.S. Open again. There's nothing like winning a Grand Slam. Serena and I, we both know that when we come out there, it's going to be two competitors competing against each other. That's just the way it is. When you walk out on the court, if you're not a competitor, you just got to go home. And we both understand that" (ASAP Sports, Venus Williams, September 8, 2001).

If the two sisters were competing with one another to see who would take the first Grand Slam title in the Williams family, it was Serena who won with her victory at the U.S. Open in 1999. Venus followed with her win at Wimbledon and then the U.S. Open the next year. When asked if it was hard for her to see her younger sister win the first Grand Slam in the family, Venus replied, "Does it really matter? She played better. It's my loss. It's her win. We won the same. It's all in the Williams family" (ASAP Sports, Venus Williams, July 1, 2000).

After winning the 2001 U.S. Open, Venus commented on the historical significance of two sisters playing one another in the finals, "We're both good athletes, that helps a lot. Then we worked hard and we believe in ourselves. That helps a lot more. Then we kind of stepped up and made it happen. That's what counts. I guess, you know, years from now we'll look back and laugh. We still laugh. But now we look back at the times that we've had before and we laugh and say, 'Boy, if I had known, I would have done better here and there.' I suppose we can keep the memory for ourselves" (ASAP Sports, Venus Williams, September 8, 2001). There would be many more laughs for them in store in the future and more history that they would make as they continued to set new records in women's tennis.

Winning a major tournament certainly was a dream for the girls from the time of their childhood on the Compton courts, and they spent their lifetime preparing for these moments. After winning the first Grand Slam tournament for the Williams family in the U.S. Open in 1999, Serena explained, "My dad used to say to Venus and I, 'Which big ones do you want to win.' I just said The Open. Venus said Wimbledon" (ASAP Sports, Serena Williams, September 11, 1999).

Yet there were some aspects of their victories that the sisters perhaps never dreamed would happen. For example, shortly after her U.S. Open victory, Serena took a phone call from President Bill Clinton while she was in the CBS studio discussing her game. "It was very exciting. I thought for sure my day couldn't get any better. Next thing I knew, someone was telling me, 'The President of the United States wants to talk.' I was thinking, 'Wow'" (ASAP Sports, Serena Williams, September 11, 1999). A reporter observed that it never happened before in women's tennis that a U.S. President called a player after a victory. To this, Serena replied, "He said that they had watched my last three matches and they were really rooting for me, him and Chelsea also. I talked to her also, she's really nice [laughter]. She said she'll show me around Stanford when I go there for Fed Cup if I wanted to. Pretty exciting" (ASAP Sports, Serena Williams, September 11, 1999).

After her victory at the U.S. Open in 2000, Venus fielded a similar call from President Clinton. After accepting his congratulations, she questioned him about traffic in New York City and the high taxes she needed to pay. Then she asked him to wish Hillary Clinton well in her upcoming race for the Senate in New York state. This was certainly a new era in women's tennis, and this point was not lost on the president or his family.

In spite of questions concerning competition on the court, the sisters competed in fun off the court as well. Serena explained, "There's a great competition going on right now with autograph signing. We're in a race. I won that one. Then the next time we were signing our doll cases. Unfortunately, the lady couldn't pass me the box in time, or else I would have won. We're tied at 1-All" (ASAP Sports, Serena Williams, September 2, 2000).

As the years passed and Venus and Serena became more dominant in the world of women's tennis, they stirred some controversy as they pressured tournament officials to be sure they were placed in different brackets when the tournament began. Such a placement arrangement would allow them the potential to face each other in an all-Williams final more regularly. In some junior tournaments, this is always the case. If two members of the same family are competing, they are always in the opposite bracket. This is not typical on the professional circuit, although Serena Williams told a reporter in an interview that she felt this should be so: "I think it should be done [putting siblings in opposing brackets], I guess, because I'm in the situation. Obviously I'm pro, I'm for that. The professionals are different from the juniors. If I really want to be on the opposite side of the draw every time, we have to see that we're 1 and 2, then forever we'll be on opposite sides of the draw. It is kind of stressful every time, I'm looking, praying. To be honest, that's my own double fault that I haven't taken the top spot, at least 1 and 2, or 3 and 4, so we're always on opposite sides" (ASAP Sports, Serena Williams, September 2, 2000). Beginning in 1999, the sisters agreed to avoid playing the same tournaments, with the exception of the Grand Slam tournaments. And when they were not competing against one another on the court, they did compete with one another as part of the Williams-Williams doubles team.

DOUBLE TROUBLE: WILLIAMS AND WILLIAMS

> We're the best doubles team America has. It would be a good pick.
>
> Venus Williams, in response to speculation that she and Serena would go to the 2000 Olympic Games as a doubles team, ASAP Sports, Venus Williams, July 7, 2000.

Doubles matches are a favorite for the Williams sisters. They won their first doubles events in 1998, one in Oklahoma and a second in Zurich,

Switzerland. Their enthusiasm for playing doubles was evident as they strode confidently on the court, smiling and waving at the crowds. At the 1999 U.S. Open, Venus explained to a reporter, "We love playing doubles. We'd never play with anyone else" (ASAP Sports, Venus Williams, September 9, 1999). And why would they? Combined they had the toughest serves, most powerful volleys, and fastest legs in tennis. The duo seemed to be undefeatable.

In their doubles play, the sisters won 10 titles at major tournaments, including Olympic gold in Australia in 2000. They also have had unique opportunities to play against tennis greats, such as Martina Navratilova. At Wimbledon in 2000, the sisters defeated DeSwardt and Navratilova. Serena explained that this was a once-in-a-lifetime opportunity, that Martina was always her favorite player. The sisters have more recently begun to turn to other partners when one of them is unable to play due to injury. Serena played doubles with Alexandra Stevenson, winning in Leipzig, Germany, in 2002, and Venus competed with Chanda Rubin at the Olympic Games in Athens, Greece, in 2004.

Serena once described to reporters the experience she had playing doubles with Venus. She explained, "It's fun because I know Venus is going to get a big first serve in. I know I just have to put it away. I'm just there. Sometimes now, my serve, I hit a big serve, she's going to put it away. Playing with her, you get to smile, not only talking about tennis. Not talking about, 'Do this, do this.' We can relax and talk about something that happened earlier in the week, whatnot. It's just so much better" (ASAP Sports, Serena Williams, July 5, 2000). For anyone watching, there was no doubt that the girls enjoyed competing together. There were frequent high fives between points and whispers when they swapped ideas about game strategies.

On the professional tour, some discussion came up about seeding the doubles tournaments. Doubles specialists, such as Rennae Stubbs, who focus primarily on their doubles play, have sometimes been quite angry that very highly seeded singles players, like Venus and Serena or Martina Hingis and Monica Seles, get top seeding in the doubles without having a good doubles ranking. When asked by a reporter to express her opinion on this, Serena seemed to think that this practice was fine and that top singles players should be able to advance in doubles tournaments. She explained, "I think it's easier for us to be seeded so the top players won't play us in the first round. That way at least we can go to the quarterfinals, so on, so forth" (ASAP Sports, Serena Williams, January 16, 2003).

Sometimes, however, it can be difficult for singles players to know whether playing doubles will take away from their singles game. Balancing the schedules for singles and doubles matches at tournaments can be quite grueling. Venus once commented on this: "And as far as doubles here [at Wimbledon], it's another kind of thing I had to do. I love the doubles, especially at Wimbledon. And I miss the doubles. And I had to play. You know, for some reason if I can't continue or if it puts me in jeopardy for my singles, I'll have to make that decision at that point. But I just had to play. Usually I start out serving, so Serena will start out serving, so I'll have to hit less serves" (ASAP Sports, Venus Williams, June 25, 2003). In 2000, Venus won both the singles and the women's doubles tournaments, putting an exclamation point on her domination at the event that year and marking the first time in tennis history that two sisters won a doubles event at Wimbledon. They repeated their victory by winning the doubles match at Wimbledon again in 2002.

In addition to playing Williams-Williams doubles matches, the sisters sometimes have paired with male players on the tour to compete in mixed doubles. Venus played with American Justin Gimelstob, and together they won the 1998 Australian Open and French Open tournaments. Serena competed with Max Mirnyi of Belarus, winning the 1998 U.S. Open and Wimbledon.

In 2004, the Williams sisters were favored to repeat their 2000 gold medal victory at the Olympic Games in Athens, Greece. However, with Serena's withdrawal from the tournament, their dream was not realized. Instead, Venus partnered in the doubles matches with Chanda Rubin (the first woman's double match she would play with a partner other than Serena). Unfortunately, the pair lost 7–5, 1–6, 6–3 during the first round to number 8 seeds Li Tang and Sun Tian Tian of China. Although some speculated that this quick loss was because she was not teamed with her sister, Venus denied these claims, insisting that she was at the event to play for the United States.

CONCLUSION

Although other sister acts had played professional tennis, professional tennis had never seen two sisters quite like Venus and Serena Williams. Eventually, Richard Williams's predictions would come true. His daughters would be ranked number 1 and 2 in the world of tennis. Venus spent 11 weeks at number 1, whereas Serena spent 57 weeks in the top spot. They had come a long way from the cracked and dangerous Compton courts, and to anyone who was watching, it was clear that they had only begun to make their mark.

Venus and Serena changed the face of women's tennis, stepping up the level of fitness, the aggressiveness of play, and the overall speed of the game. Even some of their archrivals, like Martina Hingis, admitted that they played different and better tennis when they faced Venus or Serena. Venus explained the changes she noted in her time on the tour, "I think for sure the fitness changed a lot. I think a lot of it had to do with Serena and I because, you know, I was like 16, I came out hitting these 116 [mile-per-hour] serves, running and jumping like no tomorrow, then everyone else started to realize, too, they had to up the serve and the pace. Then Serena burst on the scene and did just unbelievable things. This is always a good thing. I'm glad that I was able to be a leader in fitness and in tennis for women. I'm glad that other people have been able to take it to another level, and so will I have to keep taking it to another level to compete" (ASAP Sports, Venus Williams, June 25, 2003).

Chapter 6

CONTROVERSIES AND CHALLENGES IN TENNIS

The WTA is a close-knit community that tends to embrace its own. We've never been a part of it. But then, we never planned to be a part of them either. We're a part of ourselves.... People can criticize me and complain about me, but no one wants to see a tournament that Venus and Serena aren't in. We breathed life into this game, and people dislike us for it. But they picked the wrong family to try to tear apart.
                    Richard Williams (as quoted in Samuels, 2001)

Venus and Serena faced challenges and controversies across their lives that related to issues of race, gender, and social class that were endemic to U.S. society. Even when they were prominent tennis stars and celebrities, the Williams sisters struggled with and against issues of racism and prejudice. After the 2004 Wimbledon and U.S. Open episodes when chair umpires made mistakes that cost Venus and Serena points in their matches, Richard Williams described his daughters as the victims of a conspiracy. "Racism," he said. "It definitely has to be.... My feeling is that we've been robbed and cheated. I think it's a disgrace how the system is against those two black girls" (Berman, 2004).

Although some downplayed his assessment of what was happening by reminding him that it was because of Venus and Serena that the 2000 U.S. Open was held during prime time, the possibility that race had something to do with the calls the white umpires made was still a possibility. How could we know? And if these were racist incidents, what should be done?

"IT WAS A VERY TOUGH PUBLIC OUT THERE": ISSUES OF RACE AND RACISM

The tennis world is too white for us.... And it is ridiculous to say there is no prejudice. We are all prejudiced. America is the most prejudiced nation in the world.

Richard Williams (as quoted in Evans, 2003)

Although Venus and Serena were not the first African American women to play professional tennis, they still experienced challenges and discrimination because of their race. Their father tried to prepare them for this, even from a young age. When the girls played on the courts in Compton, he paid neighborhood kids to stand at the fence and shout obscenities and racial insults at them. He explained, "I taught them how to handle problems and solve them, to walk through them and not around them. I told them that's what rich people do.... You can't wait for a situation to happen to get ready for it" (Samuels, 2001).

There is a great deal of debate about what constitutes racism or racist practices, particularly in the United States, where color-blind policies that focus on individualism and meritocracy were increasingly becoming the norm (see Robbins, 2004). Psychologist Beverly Tatum accepted David Wellman's definition of racism as "a system of advantage based on race." This included cultural and individual messages about race, along with institutional advantages and disadvantages that could be attributed to race. Tatum explained that racism cannot be fully understood as prejudice alone, particularly if we understand prejudice as a "preconceived judgment or opinion, usually based on limited information" (Tatum, 1997, p. 5). Richard Williams, like many people, seemed to use these words interchangeably, and some even suggested that Richard was prejudiced himself as he made anti-Semitic comments and stirred controversy around race issues at various tennis venues around the world (Wertheim, 2002).

Cultural studies theorist Stuart Hall (1997) suggested that we should speak of "racisms" rather than "racism," because the concept of racisms more accurately reflects the fact that racism has specific histories that are different in various cultures and contexts. In other words, racism as it is experienced and realized in a colonized nation like Puerto Rico is different than racism as it is experienced and realized in the United States, Great Britain, or Brazil. There are different histories and contexts to racism.

This is interesting to consider in relation to Venus and Serena Williams, particularly the point about context. Venus and Serena as African American women are part of a minority culture in the United States, one that historically has experienced much discrimination and oppression, but when they travel abroad, they are perceived as part of the dominant U.S. culture. The places where they travel have different histories and manifestations of racism that may or may not overlap with the experiences Venus and Serena have had.

The tensions the sisters' positions as minorities from a dominant culture can bring were perhaps most evident at the 2003 French Open when French fans booed and jeered Serena as she played and eventually lost to Justine Henin-Hardenne in three sets. Although Oracene Price commented that the French fans had a lack of class and total ignorance, some wondered if the rift between France and the United States concerning the March 2003 invasion of Iraq had something to do with Serena's mistreatment by the fans (Watterson, 2003). Others, including Richard Williams, felt that race had something to do with the booing. Indeed, sports commentator Martin Jacques noted that neither of the sisters had much support before they reached number 1 status, and he attributed this primarily to their race and the fact that tennis was for the most part a white sport and its fans were more conservative than in other sports (Jacques, 2003). Yet, Martina Navratilova insisted that racism was not a factor, but instead, the fans were rooting for the underdog and hoping to see Serena toppled, and Tracy Austin, agreeing with Navratilova, urged Serena to see this as a compliment (Black Athlete Sports Network, 2003). Whatever the cause of the booing, Serena admitted after the match, "It was a very, very tough public out there, very tough, but that is the story of my life. I have always had to fight hard in my life and it is another battle I am going to have to win. I always try to please the crowd with my game. It's hard to fight against the whole crowd and it was not nice to hear the people applaud my mistakes" (Black Athlete Sports Network, 2003).

Richard Williams often blamed racism for Venus and Serena's alleged mistreatment on the circuit by fans and other players, but not everyone agreed. Sometimes people felt that Richard interpreted various incidents as racist, when in fact they were not. As one example, in 1997, Venus faced Irina Spirlea in a semifinal event at the U.S. Open. During a changeover in the match when the players were switching sides, Spirlea bumped into Venus at the net. Richard claimed that this was racially motivated, and that Spirlea also uttered a racial epithet when she ran into Venus. He later called Spirlea a "big, ugly, tall white turkey." Venus won the match, becoming the first unseeded player to reach a final in U.S. Open history (Berman, 2004).

Perhaps the most overtly racist incident at a major U.S. tournament happened in Indian Wells, California, in March 2001. At this event, Serena advanced to the finals when Venus withdrew from the semifinal match that pitted the sisters against one another. Venus claimed she withdrew because of injury, but some fans felt that she withdrew by order of her father, who allegedly wanted to see Serena advance to the finals. When Serena went on the court during the finals match, fans booed Serena, yelling "loser" and "cheat." Although the WTA maintained that the booing was due to Venus's last-minute withdrawal from the semifinal match, Richard claimed the booing was racist and explained in *Jet* magazine (April 9, 2001) that as he and Venus walked to their seats, people called him nigger. One man even reportedly said, "I wish it was '75; we'd skin you alive." Although no one in the crowd that day confirmed Richard's account of these events, Richard explained that he decided to handle the confrontation nonviolently, and he proceeded to his seat. He claimed that he had to hold back tears because of his treatment at this event. After Serena won the tournament, a reporter asked her whether race had anything to do with the booing she received. She replied, "Race? I think, you know, black people have been out of slavery now for just over a hundred years, and people are still kind of struggling a little bit. It hasn't been that long. I don't know if race has anything to do with this particular situation. But in general I think, yeah, there's still a little problem with racism in America" (ASAP Sports, Serena Williams, March 17, 2001).

In spite of this incident and other similar incidents, Serena reportedly did not consider tennis to be a racist sport. She told Kevin Chappell (2002) of *Ebony* magazine that television commentators and others who remark on her athleticism do so out of ignorance more than racism, largely because tennis is only partly a physical game. She explained, "Tennis is 75 percent mental. You can only get so far if you don't have it mentally. People just assume my success is all due to being athletic because maybe I'm strong-looking, but you know what they say about assumers." According to writer Jon Entine (2000), there is a trend among sports enthusiasts concerning the emphasis on black bodies over black minds (for a similar argument, see Spencer, 2004). This emphasis often echoed that of commentators like Jimmy "the Greek" Snyder, who claimed that black athletes, because of generations of slavery that purportedly paired strong black males and females to breed stronger slave children, were biologically and genetically stronger and faster, hence they were better athletes. Although he later was fired from CBS for his comments, others still believe there is truth in this claim (in spite of the fact that cultural differences in physical traits evolve over thousands of years, not just a few generations). One example of this was when African American Chicago Cubs manager

Dusty Baker, in 2003, noted that black and Hispanic players are better suited than whites to play baseball in the heat of the day.

Jon Entine, in his book *Taboo*, has proposed that differences in athletes are due to genetic predisposition. He cited the success of Kenyan marathon runners as one of many examples. To Entine, it is racist not to discuss this issue openly because it works to perpetuate myths about physical abilities and intellect. For example, there are some, like Bill Hernnstein and Charles Murray, authors of the controversial book *The Bell Curve* (1996), who have argued that intellectual capabilities are genetically predisposed, and that some races and cultures naturally will do better in intellectual endeavors than others. Entine pointed out that one of the common misconceptions about race is that someone who is physically gifted is not intellectually capable. To Entine, this is a racist myth, perpetuating a belief that black athletes are closer to animals and savages. Although Entine did not agree with Jimmy the Greek's claims about slaves being bred to be genetically stronger, he did agree that there are physical differences across races and cultures and that we need to be open and to discuss these differences so that other stereotypes, particularly about intellect, are not continued. Serena likely would agree. She once observed, "A lot of people think that black people can't rally and just think they're athletes and can't think. As you can see, that's not true. I can rally. Venus can rally" (Rineberg, 2003, p. 123). Her concern about public perceptions that African American athletes "can't think" is one shared by many who study African Americans in sport (for one discussion on this issue, see Hoberman, 1997), which negates the hard work and intellectual abilities that are required for success in professional athletics.

SELLING BLACK BODIES

From the time Venus and Serena first entered the public arena in tennis tournaments, there was no doubt they were physically different from the other players, including other African American players. In addition to their incredible athleticism and strength, they seemed to embrace their ethnicity and culture, and their hair, bound in hundreds of beads, served as one symbol of this. They never seemed to try to blend into the white culture of the sport or to look like mainstream Americans. This was a purposeful move on their parents' part. Although Richard and Oracene fully expected that their daughters would face racism as they competed in primarily white tennis venues, they did not want to negate the fact that Venus and Serena came from African American culture. Oracene explained, "I want them to know who they are and what they are. That's why I wanted them to wear beads in their hair when they first started out on tour because I felt it was important they understand where they come from. They're African American and they should be proud of it" (Hayes, 2002). Venus offered a more practical explanation for the 1,800 colored beads she wore. She told reporters, "Well, it started a long time ago when we practiced all day. We did a lot of practicing. It was not very easy to comb your hair. So my mom braided our hair, and put beads on them. Then you don't have to do it for six weeks, you don't have to do your hair every day. It's very hard. I'm not that good at doing hair, I never really learned. I guess it's my fault, but that's why—we like it. That's why I wear it" (ASAP Sports, Venus Williams, August 19, 1998).

The beads seemed to irritate some of the other players, including Venus's archrival, Martina Hingis. Early in Venus's career after Martina Hingis defeated her in straight sets in the Lipton tournament in Key Biscayne, Florida, a tennis official gave Martina one of the beads that fell from Venus's hair. During a press conference after the tournament, Hingis threw the bead at reporters, saying, "I have a present for you. One of Venus' pearls" (*Sports Illustrated* Timeline).

The beads also were of great interest to sports commentators. Mary Carillo described the beads as "noisy and disruptive," and Chris Evert said she was "tired of the beads" (Spencer, 2004). In part, this demonstrates how "sportscasters often seem challenged and mystified by what to say about them" (Daniels, as quoted in Spencer, 2004, p. 123).

From the time the girls were on the junior circuit in California, there was much interest in the sisters from various companies seeking endorsements for their products. None of the early endorsements attempted to change the image of the girls in ways that would detract from their ethnicity. There were photos of young Venus with beads in her hair modeling Reebok clothing, and there were images of Serena as a young girl sporting Puma outfits as she slammed tennis balls across the court. Some of the most prestigious and lucrative endorsements for the Williams sisters came from Reebok, Puma, Avon, Doublemint gum, McDonald's, and Wilsons Leather. All of these endorsements focused on their bodies, requiring them to sell their looks as they modeled clothing, makeup, and other products. They earned unprecedented sums of money for these contracts, a point that will be discussed in more detail in chapter 7. However, the point here is that the focus on their bodies and athleticism garnered much attention, some positively and others negatively.

Venus and Serena came into tennis during an era when many major companies believed that there would be a market among African Americans for products the sisters endorsed. In 2000, writer Julianne Malveaux estimated that the African American market was $561 billion in the United States and that this market was younger and more urban in nature than the general population. She went on to point out that Venus and Serena's charisma and visibility in the world of sport, coupled with their good looks and sense of style, did much to earn them major endorsements and contracts.

Some felt that black athletes earned special attention by virtue of the fact that they were black. Martina Navratilova, as one example, claimed that the sisters were treated with "kid gloves" because of their race. Writer Malveaux would agree, as this is a common misconception about many black professional athletes. Conservative radio talk-show host Rush Limbaugh made similar comments about black Philadelphia Eagles quarterback Donovan McNabb when he stated in 2003 that McNabb was "overrated ... what we have here is a little social concern in the NFL. The media has been very desirous that a black quarterback can do well—black coaches and black quarterbacks doing well" (Barra, 2003). The implication was that black athletes were being given a break.

Malveaux also dismissed as naive Martina Hingis's comments about endorsements going to the Williams sisters because of their race. Martina Hingis publicly complained that Venus and Serena earned endorsements because they were black, and she used this as an example of how racism was not a problem in tennis because their race was benefiting them financially and otherwise. After the 2001 U.S. Open when a reporter asked Serena her response to Hingis's comment, she replied, "I think in a sport that is a predominantly white sport, I think when athletes—when people see new faces, like for instance golf with Tiger Woods, maybe if hockey were to have a superstar that was maybe Spanish or maybe black, I think then maybe it would get a few more people to watch a sport. But as for being black and getting more endorsements because I'm black, I wouldn't know anything about that. All I know is I get endorsements because I win and I work hard. I go out there and have a good attitude and I smile. I like tennis. Whether I got endorsements or not, I don't know. All I know is that that's what I can say about it" (ASAP Sports, Serena Williams, August 27, 2001). Malveaux likely would agree with Serena's observation. She pointed out that among U.S. companies, decisions are made based on profit, and because Venus and Serena would "sell," they were offered large endorsement contracts.

In early 2001, Play Along Toys, a Florida company, paid Venus and Serena $125,000 each to use their likenesses to make dolls. The production of the dolls revealed much about the ways in which their images were marketed and why. When the dolls were first produced, Venus was at the top of the professional tennis world. Los Angeles *Times* staff writer Ralph Frammolino reported that when the first batch was issued in 2001, there were two Venus dolls for every Serena doll shipped to retailers. A year later, as the sisters' tennis playing became increasingly on the same level, they were marketed evenly. By the third year, the dolls were canceled because of the slumping economy. However, Jay Freeman, president of the company, explained that they probably would have reversed the trend in the third year, marketing two Serena dolls for every Venus doll. Such a change indicated the change in status of the two sisters in tennis. Freeman explained that children always want to buy the winner.

The selling of black youth culture was increasingly prominent throughout the United States during the 1990s and 2000s. There were films that glorified the experiences of young blacks, various forms of rap and hip-hop and the corresponding artifacts that commodified black experiences, and increasing media attention, both positive and otherwise, that portrayed black youth in ways that made them appear to be a seductive object of either fear or desire. Writer S. Craig Watkins (1999) pointed out some of the challenges for young black youth during the latter part of the twentieth century, particularly in relation to the inundation of media images. For one, Watkins found it to be of great irony that "at the same time black youth are so prominently figured in the nation's war on drugs, the largest prison industrial complex buildup in history, and tightening welfare restrictions, they are equally prominent in the marketing of $100 athletic shoes, the corporatization of collegiate athletics, and the breaking of new trends to a robust youth consumer economy" (pp. 1–2). This tension was even evident in the Williams family as Oracene's oldest daughter, Yetunde, and Richard's first wife and children lived in the ghetto, whereas Venus and Serena went on to find fortune as they marketed expensive athletic clothing and gear. Watkins asked, "How do [black youth] grapple with a social, economic, and political world that, on the one hand, is becoming increasingly hostile toward them yet, on the other, has developed a voracious appetite for the cultural products and performances created by black youth?" (p. 2).

In addition to breaking new ground in sports because they were African American, Venus and Serena moved the world of women's tennis into a new arena with their power and athleticism. Because of this, there were controversies due to their gender in relation to societal expectations about what it means to be a woman.

WALK LIKE A LADY

During the 2003 Australian Open, Oracene told a reporter for the *International Herald Tribune*, "[The public and the fans] seem to accept Tiger

[Woods] a little better than the girls, you know what I'm saying? He's a man." She added, "They don't need women showing so much strength or how powerful they can be or how they can think." Price said she believed that there was also a racial component at work, suggesting that there were no complaints when Martina Navratilova and Chris Evert were dominating women's tennis to much the same degree as her daughters do now (*International Herald Tribune*, 2003). This last point concerning Navratilova and Evert is certainly debatable. Martina Navratilova received much scrutiny in the press because of her appearance, her hard-hitting style, and her lesbianism, and she often felt that the more glamorous Evert earned endorsements from companies like Lipton Tea because her image was considered to be more appealing to the U.S. public. However, some feel it is more difficult for fans to warm up to those women players who break the mold, pointing out that neither Navratilova nor Evert, who initially was dubbed "The Ice Maiden," were warmly received by the fans and media until they began to lose matches and show their human fallibility (see Black Athlete Sports Network, 2003).

In addition to these more subtle perceptions of women, particularly African American women's roles in sport, there have been some overtly racist comments made about the two sisters' bodies by sports commentators. New York sportscaster Sid Rosenberg appeared on the June 5, 2001, Don Imus show and complained about the sisters' athletic appearance. Rosenberg stated, "I can't even watch them play anymore. I find it disgusting. I find both of those, what do you want to call them—they're just too muscular. They're boys. . . . One time my friend, he goes, 'Listen one of these days you're going to find Venus and Serena Williams in *Playboy*.' I said, 'You got a better shot at *National Geographic*.'" Rosenberg was fired for his comments but later rehired after he issued a public apology on the air, stating simply, "I want to extend my most sincere apologies to [them] and to anybody else who was offended by my remarks" (*Jet*, July 9, 2001).

Some people seemed to have problems with the sisters' demeanor on and off the court. John McEnroe was particularly critical of what he considered to be their arrogance. The irony of such an observation from the "Superbrat" was not lost on reporters. When asked by a reporter about such criticisms, and whether these were proffered because of the sisters' accomplishments, Serena replied, "You know, I think maybe because there's a lot of guys out there who have—I don't know what—you know, just say a lot of things. If a lady comes out and says it, it's totally different. If a guy says it, it's acceptable, it's okay. But that's life. That's life" (ASAP Sports, Serena Williams, June 28, 2000).

As Venus and Serena rose to the top of the game, there was speculation concerning how good they really were. In other words, some wanted to see them play against men, as though that would solidify the fact they were really dominant athletes. Donald Trump offered $1 million for John McEnroe to play one of the sisters, reviving discussions of a renewed Battle of the Sexes with a match between the Williams sisters and the McEnroe brothers, John and Patrick. In part, this proposal began with speculation concerning whether the sisters could win on the men's circuit. McEnroe claimed they could not beat even a college male player.

This discussion of women competing against men in athletics certainly is not new. The possibility of a Williams-McEnroe event evoked memories of Billie Jean King's Battle of the Sexes match against Bobby Riggs in 1973 (6–4, 6–3, 6–3). A similar proposal offering $2 million was made in 1992 for Monica Seles, then the top-ranked player, to compete against Jimmy Connor, then ranked 46th and 21 years her senior. Seles declined.

In 2002, Women Sports Zone, Inc., filed a lawsuit against the Williams sisters, claiming they pulled out of a contract for the Battle of the Sexes II, which would have pitted the sisters against the McEnroe brothers. The company estimated that the profit from the event would have reached $45 million.

Of course Venus and Serena did compete with men all the time, but this competition was out of the public eye. Their hitting coaches were sometimes men, and they even competed against the German Karsten Braasch in 1998. Braasch, who was known to be eccentric and to smoke cigarettes as soon as his match was finished, defeated both sisters in separate matches, even though years later Venus and Serena denied that the matches ever took place (Flatman, 2003).

In addition to questions concerning the sisters' ability to compete against men, there were controversies around pay equity on the professional tennis tour. A reporter asked Venus at the 2002 Wimbledon tournament, "If it came down to playing these three-set matches, making less than the men here, or playing five-set matches which would give them no excuse but to pay you the same, which would you choose?" Venus replied, "I would choose that they play three-set matches." When the reporter asked if she thought women should then make less money, Venus responded, "No, not at all. I think it's hard to always change minds. But in my opinion it's unacceptable in the workplace. Outside of tennis, it's against the law, I'm not sure in England—I would think so—to pay a woman less. That's what I think. I'm a woman, but also I try to be fair in all my views. The last word is it should be three sets for the men." The reporter closed by asking, "Do you like watching three-out-of-five-set matches with the guys sometimes?" to which Venus answered, "I don't really watch men's tennis. I watch the women" (ASAP Sports, Venus Williams, June 29, 2002).

Oracene Price likely agreed with her daughter. She felt there were too many chauvinistic attitudes against women, particularly those involved in sports. She said, "It's amazing that girls on the Tour don't think they deserve more money. That's a shame, because to be perfectly honest, when I bump into people they tell me that men's tennis makes them turn off their TV. Women are the ones keeping tennis interesting at the moment and yet they are the ones being penalized for that" (Hayes, 2002). Her comments were confirmed by the increased attendance and viewing audiences for the WTA. From 1998 to 1999, there was a 13 percent increase in the number of spectators at tournament events worldwide, and 2000 brought five new events, $3 million more in prize money, and increased viewing audiences on television networks like ESPN. Many sportswriters attributed this boom in women's tennis to the glamour and celebrity that surrounded its stars. The women on the tour were charismatic, and some worried that all the attention directed toward them was because of the hype and not the sport (see Hruby, 2000). Anna Kournikova was perhaps the biggest anomaly as she earned some of the largest endorsement contracts in the history of women's tennis without ever winning a Grand Slam or other major tournament in the sport.

In 2001, Richard Williams proposed that his daughters were entitled to a cut of the Sanex WTA Tour's revenue. Richard argued that because the television ratings were high when his daughters played, and that these ratings benefited the tour, Venus and Serena should make more money. However, the WTA did not operate this way, and it likely never will. Instead, according to *Tennis* magazine writer Sally Jenkins (2001), players join the WTA and agree to set aside a certain amount of self-interest to benefit the tour, which in turn must deal with other costs and liabilities that include securing corporate sponsorship, selling TV rights, booking the arenas, and making sure the extra bleachers needed for events are well constructed according to city codes. Jenkins argued that Venus and Serena could make more money simply by playing more tennis. In 2000, she noted that Venus played 10 tournaments and Serena played 11. That same year, Lindsay Davenport played 18 and Martina Hingis played 20. Jenkins noted that, had Venus and Serena played as much tennis as Davenport and Hingis, they could have nearly doubled their earnings from tennis.

In addition to their tremendous influence among African American men and women in the United States, the Williams family hoped to empower and change lives for African women in many countries across the continent. Oracene explained, "In the few schemes that have been started in Africa, women are never the priority. Whether it be in education or the workplace, women are barely considered. That's why this program is so close to my and my girls' heart. It's time for change" (Hayes, 2002). Oracene, along with Venus and Serena, planned to visit South Africa, Ghana, and the Ivory Coast to promote tennis among African women.

"SO LET'S DO BATTLE"

Venus and Serena's drive and competitive spirit were undeniable. When Serena was asked what gave her the greatest joy about being a tennis player, she explained, "Holding up a trophy at the end of a tournament. It's the best. For me it's a great feeling. I really—I don't know. I'm really competitive. I like to win a lot. When I'm able to hold up that trophy, it's a great feeling for me" (ASAP Sports, Serena Williams, September 2, 2000).

Venus likewise seemed to enjoyed the competitiveness and victories of tennis. At the 2000 U.S. Open, Venus explained, "I feel like I deserve to be No. 1. I think somewhat this is the most fun part of tennis, when you see yourself moving ahead, you're working hard, getting the results. Back when I was 200, it was just nice to go to 110, 86. This is the most fun part, and maybe the most difficult, because you have to play more consistently. I'm a couple thousand points behind the No. 1 player at this point, but that's okay. I'm moving forward the best I can" (ASAP Sports, Venus Williams, September 3, 2000).

In spite of the fame, fortune, and pressures of being African American women in tennis, Venus and Serena seemed to handle their lives and the expectations of them with grace, and they strove to move forward in the world of women's tennis and elsewhere. Even Martina Navratilova, who tended to downplay the effects of race and racism on Venus's and Serena's careers and lives overall, conceded, "God knows that African Americans have a big bone to pick with white people. I've seen it myself. You can really have a chip on your shoulder. I think they [the Williams] have handled it really well" (Vecsey, 2002).

Journalist George Vecsey (2002) noted that black fans were celebrating Venus's and Serena's victories in much the same way that people did when Jackie Robinson was playing baseball, but that the constituency supporting the Williams sisters went well beyond a black fan base, extending into the mainstream United States. Indeed, Serena explained, "A lot of people come up to me and don't ask for my autograph, they just say thanks. It's a really special feeling. It's been happening a lot lately. And it's not just Blacks" (Chappell, 2002).

After Venus's Wimbledon win in 2000, a reporter commented on the excitement that her victory, coupled with Serena's U.S. Open win the year before, caused among people of color, asking if she realized this impact. Venus replied, "We're really aware of that. We know the black people are really top supporters. When you go to Germany, the Germans support the Germans. We really relate to each other, of course. We're black. We fought for everything we have…. People are turning their TV and suddenly they see this black girl playing tennis" (ASAP Sports, Venus Williams, July 8, 2000).

In addition to expanding the fan base through the African American community and television viewing audience, more young black children began to play tennis, and many directly attributed this interest to Venus and Serena. L. Jon Wertheim (2004) reported in *Sports Illustrated* that even if the sisters' dominance in women's tennis ended with their loss at the U.S. Open in 2004, their impact on the sport would continue to be profound. By 2004, USTA president Alan Schwartz encouraged multicultural participation in tennis, something that would have been highly unlikely before Venus and Serena dominated the sport. Schwartz even provided help for those players who needed financial support for their endeavors. Wertheim quoted Scoville Jenkins, one of the up-and-coming young black stars, who noted the effect the Williams sisters had on him. Jenkins said, "I think every African-American has been inspired by them. We all grew up seeing how well they did, and we wanted to be like them" (Wertheim, 2004). Wertheim contended that the sisters gave tennis an element of "street cred," making it acceptable for young black kids to be seen playing tennis (Wertheim, 2004).

A reporter at the 1999 U.S. Open asked Venus about her influence on young African Americans: "Could you talk about your impact on attracting African American kids to the game? Several inner cities have shown tennis programs expanding. Kids are looking up to you." Venus replied, "We definitely have a large impact. Before, you never see that many black people at a tennis match. Like today, there were quite a few there. In the past, two or three years ago, it wasn't happening. People are watching what Serena and I do. I guess they want to be a part of it" (ASAP Sports, Venus Williams, August 30, 1999). Serena had similar thoughts. She told a reporter how she and Venus had an incredible influence on kids who came from the inner city, in part because they had the same background. She explained, "I think that it really helps people believe that, you know what, 'If they did it, I can, too.' I think it's just really great. And I feel honored that I was chosen to have an opportunity to be that role model for those people in the inner city and the inner communities, and just for them to realize, 'You know, Serena did it. You can do it too.' I didn't have this, I didn't have that, but I did it, and you can do it too.... I just see it all around. I mean, when I meet some parents, and they'll say, 'You know, my child is doing A, B, C, and D because of you.' For someone older to come up to me and say, 'I started my kid, not necessarily tennis, but being a better individual, trying to get better grades because of what you and your sister have done,' ... I really, really appreciate that because it makes me realize that, you know, people really do look up to me and they really appreciate some stuff that we've done" (ASAP Sports, Serena Williams, June 22, 2004). By 2004, Venus and Serena's impact on future tennis stars was beginning to become apparent. Angela Haynes was a promising talent for the women's tour, and Scoville Jenkins and Donald Young were making their mark on the men's junior tour. Their impact on other aspects of young people's lives was more difficult to quantify, yet it seems the influence was real.

In spite of all the challenges and controversies that have swirled around their lives on and off the tennis court, Venus and Serena still seemed to be committed to staying on top in the sport. Venus once explained, "I've never had a goal to have all the Grand Slam titles, more than anyone, more than Margaret Court. I've just had a goal to play good tennis as long as I can" (ASAP Sports, Venus Williams, September 9, 2000). By 2004, it seemed she was still committed to this idea. Venus still named tennis as her top priority, explaining of any up-and-coming new tennis star, "So let's do battle. I still want to be the best" (Tresniowski and Rozsa, 2004). As might be expected, Serena seemed to share her sister's goal.

Chapter 7

CELEBRITY, FASHION, AND BEYOND

In 1990, Venus was featured in the *New York Times* with a headline that read, "Status: Undefeated, Future: Rosy, Age 10." Nine months later, she appeared in a front-page story in which she told reporters she wanted to be an astronaut. Clearly she had hopes and aspirations that moved well beyond the world of tennis from the time she was a child. The same was true for Serena, who once reported that she wanted to be a veterinarian. Although their goals and aspirations certainly have evolved over the years, the one constant in their lives has been tennis. However, they both made their marks in areas off the court, including modeling and endorsement contracts, fashion and design, and acting.

Venus and Serena sometimes have been subject to criticism because they have a life beyond tennis, but even this seemed to be part of Richard Williams's master plan. Serena told Oprah Winfrey, "We like to have different interests ... because we get bored really quick ... but a lot of players, they have just myopic views ... but we like to do different things, because tennis can only last so long.... Our parents never wanted us to be like that. We've always had things to fall back on. We went to school" (Harpo, 2002). Because they always had a sense that their tennis careers could last only a brief time, they extended their careers off the court as they earned celebrity in different venues.

CELEBRITY

It was not long into their professional careers that the sisters faced consequences, both good and bad, for being famous. After Venus's second victory at Wimbledon, a reporter asked whether she liked the kind of ce-lebrity that came with playing tennis. Venus replied, "I like the upgrades, special privileges and things like that. But other than that, no. I'm just trying to be me." The reporter followed Venus's response by asking when she found celebrity to be difficult. Venus explained, "Really, just every day, you know, going to the supermarket. If I want to get an ice cream, if I want to go to the health food store, if I want to go to the mall, or if I want to go to Blockbuster, just things like that. I just like to be solitary, just me and my little dog, we go everywhere" (ASAP Sports, Venus Williams, July 8, 2001).

Serena faced similar challenges, and she admitted that she did not read the articles written about her in the press. She candidly told reporters who questioned her about this, "At the beginning, I was caught up with reading all the articles about myself. It kind of got me a little messed up in the mind. I began to expect too much of myself because I was reading what everyone else thought. I was thinking, 'Wow, you know, maybe I need to think this.' I just got a little bit crazy. Now I just don't read it. I'm sorry" (ASAP Sports, Serena Williams, July 27, 2001). Just a year later, she found that she was facing daily drawbacks attributable to her celeb-rity: "I couldn't imagine my life getting any crazier. I can't go anywhere, especially in America. It's very difficult for me to go anywhere—even to the local grocery store. I can't go because people are always really excited to see me ... ever since I became No. 2 maybe it's gotten worse. I wouldn't know because it's been like this for a long time now.... I feel like people are always staring at me. But, you know, you always get used to it. You feel all eyes on you. I've really gotten used to it in the past. Now obviously maybe it's a bit more. If it is a bit more, it's maybe just a little bit because I was pretty far out there in the media. I've always been doing pretty well" (ASAP Sports, Serena Williams, June 24, 2002).

For Serena, this celebrity became more than a nuisance. There were some unsettling consequences to her fame. Throughout 2002, Albrecht Stromeyer, a German who claimed that he loved her and would never hurt her, stalked Serena at various tennis events around the world. He was arrested in England in July 2002 and then again just a month later in Flushing, New York, at the National Tennis Center. In a written state-ment, Stromeyer claimed that he was following Serena around the world. He had been asked to leave the Italian Open and Wimbledon that same year, and he reportedly was seen at the French Open and in a tournament in Berlin (Crockett, 2002). He also tried to find Serena at her hotel in Scottsdale, Arizona. After hearing of Stromeyer's arrest while she played a semifinal match at Wimbledon, ESPN.com reported that Serena commented, "I don't really pay any attention to anything like that.... But I don't see how it could affect my game, him being arrested. I'm a strong person. I try not to let things like that affect me.... I'm not afraid but I'm cautious. It might be scary sometimes, but I have to live my life. As popularity grows, there is a price you pay. But I'd prefer to be a successful person than turn away from that because it has a personal price tag on it" (Garber, 2002).

Other women tennis players have faced similar threats, including Martina Hingis and Jennifer Capriati. Most alarming was when Monica Seles was attacked and stabbed by Guenter Parche, a deranged stalker who apparently was interested in Steffi Graf. As Seles took a break while playing a quarterfinal match in Germany in 1993, Parche approached her from behind and stabbed her with a kitchen knife. She suffered a half-inch wound in her back and shock, but fortunately the injury, although terrible, was not life-threatening. In spite of this, Seles understandably struggled to recover from the trauma of the event. Some commentators claimed the increased attention to women in sports, the emphasis on fashion and styles the women wore, and the celebrity that accompanied their athletic accomplishments all may have contributed to this chilling trend (Brennan, as quoted in Garber, 2002). Serena decided to hire a security guard who accompanied her to matches. She was not alone in such a decision. Several other players at major events were accompanied by security guards, and some hired as many as three or four escorts.

As their celebrity and recognition grew, Venus and Serena were considered to be crossover pop-culture stars. This meant that they were famous in areas that crossed traditional boundaries. They were not just tennis stars; they also were models, designers, actors, and more. The sisters had a Sega video game based on their tennis playing, and they appeared on television, in magazines, and in film. Their pictures began to appear on the front pages of tabloids and across the Internet. Thier television appearances included 10 episodes of *Hollywood Squares* in 1999, and several talk shows, including *The Oprah Winfrey Show* and CBS's *Late Show with David Letterman*. On August 28, 2003, the sisters co-presented Best Male Video for the MTV Video Music Awards. More recently, they have been the subject of biographical television shows. In May 2004, E! cable network aired a 60-minute *True Hollywood Story: The Williams Sisters* based on their lives. Venus and Serena's fan base clearly extended well beyond traditional tennis fans, and people the world over recognized them only by their first names. Seventy-two percent of the population recognized Serena in 2003, and 73 percent recognized Venus (Rovell, 2003).

Serena commented once on what it was like to be a crossover pop star: "All the time I'm like in one of those US publications every week now, whether it's *People, Us,* or *In Touch.* I can count on being in there every week. It's like, 'What did I do this week? What did they come up to say this week?' I think that's when you really know you're a crossover celebrity, when you're always in that" (ASAP Sports, Serena Williams, June 22, 2004).

Some reporters felt that Venus and Serena's celebrity and success did a lot to draw other celebrities to the game of tennis. Brandy, Gladys Knight, P. Diddy, Lennox Lewis, and others attended tennis matches when Venus and Serena were playing. One reporter observed to Venus, "It seems like in the last two, three years, more entertainers and athletes are coming to see you and Serena specifically, especially at the big events. Is that great to see? Does that give you a sense of pride? Do you think you and Serena are Tiger-izing the game?" To this, Venus replied, "I guess they come because they've heard a lot and they want to see what's going on.... You know, I think it's nice. I think it's very exciting that people are coming out from all walks of life to come see us. It's not only us, it's other players, too, in my opinion. I think it's especially exciting, especially here at The Open, the place to be during these two weeks" (ASAP Sports, Venus Williams, September 5, 2001).

In spite of the drawbacks of celebrity, the sisters have benefited from their fame, particularly through record-breaking endorsement deals. Their celebrity made them prime candidates for contracts that would allow them to sell products for large companies. Venus and Serena earned the highest endorsement contracts of any African American woman in sports history.

LAND OF NO RETURNS:
MAJOR ENDORSEMENT CONTRACTS

Venus's celebrity began to grow when she was between 10 and 14, a relatively dormant time of her tennis career. During this period, she found herself on the front page of the *New York Times,* in *Sports Illustrated,* and on national news. People saw much potential in her athleticism, and they seemed to be drawn to her story as she worked her way from the ghetto tennis courts in Compton, California, to become a major player in the world of tennis.

At 15, Venus signed a five-year $12 million contract with Reebok. With this deal, she represented the company both as a model and as spokesperson. She wore Reebok clothes at tennis events, and she allowed her image to be used in advertisements for the company. This change in the family's financial situation enabled the Williams family to move to a 10-acre estate in Palm Beach Gardens, Florida. This was a historic deal, with record-breaking money going to a child athlete who had not even played a professional tournament. Richard had a hand in the deal, and he helped to negotiate the contract as several companies pursued young Venus.

In 1998, Serena followed in her sister's footsteps when she secured a $12 million endorsement over five years with Puma. Unlike Venus, Serena's contract came with some caveats. To retain the deal, Serena, who was not a top tennis seed at the time, needed to find her way into the top 10 players. She met this demand 15 months after signing the contract, and due to Richard's foresight in negotiating the contract, she earned bonuses when she cracked the top 10, causing the endorsement earnings to rise to $13 million.

After the Reebok and Puma contracts, many endorsements followed. After Venus won the 2000 Wimbledon and U.S. Open, she signed a $40-million agreement with Reebok, the single largest endorsement ever earned by a female athlete. By 2002, Venus was one of the wealthiest women in the history of U.S. sports, with an estimated worth close to $100 million. Serena was not far behind. Her estimated worth was $60 million. Additional endorsements for Venus and Serena came from Avon, Wrigley gum, American Express, Wilsons Leather, Nike, Wilson tennis racquets, McDonald's, and Unilever Close-up toothpaste. These agreements allow the companies to use Venus and Serena as tools to market their products around the world.

Endorsements for the Williams sisters, like other areas of their lives and careers, have not been without controversy. Perhaps one of the most troubling endorsements was when the sisters appeared in a "Got Milk" ad for the National Dairy Council, sporting the now-famous milk moustaches that have been worn by many celebrities. Ethical questions about their participation in this advertisement have been raised. For example, Venus told reporters at the 2002 Wimbledon that she did not drink milk (ASAP Sports, Venus Williams, July 4, 2002). In fact, the National Dairy Council reported that approximately 75 percent of African Americans are lactose intolerant and, like Venus, cannot drink milk. This raises questions about why the girls, who were making millions of dollars in other endorsement deals, would agree to do this ad. Of course, they were not the only African Americans who participated in the Got Milk campaign. Marion Jones, Tyra Banks, rap star Nelly, and film director Spike Lee also were photographed with the famous milk moustache. The ad campaign had wide visibility and circulation.

Other endorsement contracts for Venus and Serena came with interesting obligations. For example, their endorsement with Doublemint gum included participation in the Doublemint A.C.E. grant. This grant allowed the sisters to recognize college students and student service organizations for distinctive contributions to campuses or communities.

In all, Venus and Serena combined have earned more than $26 million in prize money during their professional tennis careers, and their endorsements have brought in millions more. Although this was certainly a great deal of money, it was significantly less than top male athletes. Tiger Woods made more than $80 million in 2003, as did race car driver Michael Schumacher. *Forbes* magazine writer Kurt Bandenhausen (2004) noted that although there were still many inequities in pay between men's and women's sports, tennis was one of the few women's sports in which women had the potential to match men in endorsements. However, he pointed out that Venus and Serena had not realized the income they thought they would from these endorsements. Bandenhausen explained that Serena's deal with Nike did not come close to the published $60 million because her injuries and the fact that she did not play many tournaments each year led Nike to sign her for much less (about $4 million a year). To increase her earnings from endorsements, Bandenhausen explained that Serena needed to return to her status as a top player. Bandenhausen made similar arguments about Venus's potential earnings, claiming that her latest Reebok deal was worth only $21 million over five years, rather than the $40 million that initially was publicized. He also noted that it may be difficult for Venus and Serena to renew these contracts when they expire because their status and visibility in the game was waning, and there was a general perception that it would be harder for them to "move product."

In spite of this decline in their potential earnings, there was no doubt that Venus and Serena made unprecedented money in tennis and endorsement contracts. A 2004 American Express ad stated, "Welcome to Venus, Land of No Returns, Official Card of Heavy Hitters." This seemed to say it all.

TRENDSETTING STYLE AND THE WORLD OF FASHION

Both Venus and Serena believed that looking good was a top priority, and they gained much attention for their ability to be trendsetters in the world of style and fashion, both on and off the court. Serena was named a fashion trendsetter in the October 21, 2002, issue of *People* magazine, and she was featured as fashion icon in the January 2004 issue of *Vogue Italia*.

Venus always seemed to attend to her clothes, and it seemed to be a natural decision for her to go into the world of clothing design. She explained, "I like to have the complete outfit. I just believe that if you look good, you play better. I'm serious. Have you ever gone anywhere, you're not looking your best, you feel a little, you know, a little self-conscious. When I walk out on that court, my game's ready and outfit's ready, too [laughing]" (ASAP Sports, Venus Williams, January 20, 2004).

Venus and Serena both liked to accessorize their outfits on and off the court. Serena wore gold sparkles to add some pizzazz to the white Wimbledon suit, and she has sported gold shoes, a diamond tiara, and rhinestones that were hand sewn onto her tennis outfits. Before her second round at the U.S. Open in 2004, Serena asked a judge to retrieve her purse from the locker room. She realized she had forgotten her earrings, and she wanted to wear them when she played. She explained, "I like to look good when I go out to play. I felt like I was missing an element. I like to wear heavy earrings.... I just—I really believe in accessorizing. I used to wear lots of bracelets. Now I only have the one bracelet on. I have a ring. I like to have my earrings and necklace. I just like to accessorize on the court. I think it's important for me to look the best I can. I mean most people see me on the tennis court, and a lot of people don't see me elsewhere. That's where I'm mostly photographed at" (ASAP Sports, Serena Williams, September 1, 2004). Venus agreed with Serena that accessorizing is important. Venus claimed, "Earrings, I got these in Hong Kong. I guess accessorize, accessorize, accessorize. I'm just your regular girl, I really am" (ASAP Sports, Venus Williams, January 20, 2004).

Venus began to be involved with clothing design when she helped to create her own line of clothing for Wilsons Leather, and she proudly modeled some of her clothing when she appeared on *The Oprah Winfrey Show* in 2002. Designing seemed to be something she thought about and enjoyed a great deal. She once explained, "I'll be asleep or something, and I'll get an idea for a shirt or a dress, so I'll get up and sketch it out" (Aronson, 2001, p. 41). Venus later worked with Reebok and Diane von Furstenberg to design tennis dresses, and she designed a hat for McDonald's for the 2004 Olympic Games in Athens, Greece. As she explained, "Someone from marketing McDonald's suggested it. So I had a few drafts and a few rejects [laughter]. Just like anything else. But eventually it came out with the right design. So it was somewhat of a last-minute thing. It was I guess in about March, which was what, six months or so, so it took a while before I got the right design.... Actually, I was very nervous because designing for McDonald's, a huge worldwide corporation, it was intimidating. I kind of stalled a little bit. I kept not thinking about it, not thinking about it.

Finally I had to do it. So it was a different kind of pressure, different kind of experience" (ASAP Sports, Venus Williams, August 15, 2004).

Serena launched her own clothing label called Aneres (her named spelled backward) in 2003, and her sisters Venus and Lyndrea, along with her friend and singer Brandy, were among those wearing her clothes. Serena used fashion magazines along with pictures of pop culture to help with some of her design ideas. In 2004, Serena earned more publicity for her design when Miss New Jersey wore an Aneres dress in the Miss America pageant.

Outside of clothing design, Venus launched her own full-service interior design firm called V Starr Interiors. The company, based in Jupiter, Florida, specialized in residential and commercial design. V Starr helped to design the set for the PBS show *The Tavis Smiley Show*. The motto for her company was "Your wish is our design." When asked if clients asked for her autograph, Venus replied, "No one has. Most people, you know, if they do call my office, if they're confident enough to call, they have to give myself and my company enough trust that I can do their home, that I can be able to make their dreams come true in their home. So there's a certain amount of trust there already, so they're not really after the autograph. Sure, they're, you know, hopefully excited about my play and my accomplishments in tennis. But other than that, I'm also serious about the design" (ASAP Sports, Venus Williams, January 13, 2003).

Venus and her interior design firm V Starr Interiors hoped to secure New York City as the site for the 2012 Olympic Games. To help prepare the city for this bid, Venus designed model apartments for the Olympic Village. Although she expressed her hope to play in the games, she realized that this might be a long shot because she would be 32 years old in 2012; however, she had a terrific experience with the Olympics and wanted to continue her involvement.

BEYOND

Venus and Serena certainly will have a long-lasting impact on U.S. culture and international sport because they are role models both on and off the court. Serena explained, "Well, I think a lot of young African Americans, young black people, definitely look up to myself and Venus, even Marian Jones, a lot of other prominent black athletes out there. I don't feel pressure to be like kind of in a tense situation, be uptight and a little bit nervous, because I think I am a role model, but at the same time I'm not out there doing things that would make—that I don't want kids seeing me do. I'm not out there doing those type of things. So for me it's easy. For me, I'm just going out there, playing tennis. I know I'm just going to have a good attitude, no matter what happens, I'm going to have fun, I'm going to smile and I'm going to enjoy myself. That's natural for me. So I don't feel pressure. Hopefully kids can learn from me that, you know, if you just live a good life.... I think I've had a strong spiritual background also, and that helped me out a lot. So for me, I don't feel pressure on being a role model or having black kids look up to me" (ASAP Sports, Serena Williams, September 2, 2001). Although Serena may have appeared non-chalant concerning her position in U.S. culture and sport history, she and Venus undoubtedly had achieved a status few female African American athletes before them could claim. Any kid could admire and learn from much about their lives, not the least of which was their ability to handle fame with grace and humility.

Chapter 8

HOW BIG A DEAL IT IS

I've been saying they're like Muhammad Ali: you'll only know
how big a deal it was years and years from now.

> Oracene Price at the 2001 U.S. Open
> (as quoted in Wertheim, 2002)

Muhammad Ali was an African American heavyweight boxing champion and Olympic gold medalist who began life named Cassius Clay. He was born in Louisville, Kentucky, in 1942, just a month before Venus and Serena's father, Richard, was born. Clay converted to Islam in 1967, and he changed his name to Muhammad Ali to reflect his new faith. His heavyweight championship was revoked that same year when he refused to serve with the U.S. military in Vietnam. Ali was known for verbally taunting his opponents, skillfully using rhyming insults and "playing the dozens." Ali marked a new role for black athletes in relation to the media and the general public as he made bold assertions about black pride. The 1960s and 1970s did not provide a safe haven of racial tolerance for African Americans in sport, as Ali observed when he noted that as a black man he would not be able to order a cheeseburger in a restaurant in Louisville, even with his gold medal hanging around his neck (Entine, 2000). Muhammad Ali was more political than any other African American athlete of his time, particularly as he voiced his strong opposition to the Vietnam War. He was outspoken and flamboyant during a time when African Americans in sport were expected to be dutiful, modest, and respectful of white authority (Hauser, 1991). However, as Hoberman (1997) pointed out, there has been a hiatus in black athletes' involvement in racial politics and political activity since Muhammad Ali. The Williams sisters are no exception to this.

Oracene Price's comparison of her daughters to Muhammad Ali provides an interesting commentary on the role Venus and Serena have played, and may continue to play, in U.S. society. Like Ali, these girls have broken new ground in the world of sport. What is left to be seen, however, is whether they will have the staying power that Ali had and whether they will take the initiative to influence political and cultural aspects of U.S. life, particularly around issues of race.

"THE BEST EVER IN THE HISTORY OF THE GAME"

Richard Williams has been known to say that he would like his daughters to quit playing tennis by the time they are 24 or 25 years old because he believes they can do many other things. As early as 1999 speculation flew that Venus would retire by the time she was 20. By 2004, Venus and Serena were ranked 9th and 8th, respectively, by the WTA. Neither had won a major tournament in more than a year, and both were plagued with injuries. Venus suffered from an abdominal strain and wrist problems, and Serena struggled to overcome her knee injury. Their playing was inconsistent and plagued with unforced errors, and they needed much improvement to their game in order to remain contenders in the sport.

In spite of the fact that the sisters' reign in the world of women's tennis seemed to be waning, their future in the sport was very much in their own hands. Both women were athletic and powerful enough to return to top positions in the sport if they wished. Their ground strokes and serves were still among of the most powerful in the sport, and their athleticism and talent were still largely unmatched. What seemed to be missing were the drive and determination to win, and many wondered whether their heart was still in the game.

Richard still seemed to have a tremendous influence on his daughters, but they were now grown women and making decisions on their own. It may be difficult to predict when they might leave the tennis courts to pursue their other interests. In 2003, Venus and Serena predicted they would stay in the game for another decade, into their early thirties, and Venus wished they would retire together. Yet, at the end of 2004, Venus did not qualify for the year-end WTA championships. Billie Jean King noted that Venus still seemed to be unable to find the form that had taken her to Wimbledon victories in 2000 and 2001.

Some questioned Venus's motivation and wondered if she had lost her competitive edge. In all fairness, it was her father's dream she was chasing, at least in part. He was the one who took her to the tennis court when she was four years old, putting her on the path that would take her to the top of the game. And, at least for a time, it seemed that tennis would be her dream, too. In 2001, Venus explained, "When I was younger, I played tennis because my parents wanted me to. I was happy doing it. I never thought twice about it. And I suppose later on, as I got older and was able to understand and I kind of understood what was going on around me, that's when I decided or I understood that, 'Hey, I wanted to be a player, too'" (ASAP Sports, Venus Williams, September 8, 2001). However, by 2004 she seemed to have other dreams. What remained to be seen was how long she would want to be a player and whether or not she would continue to be a top competitor in the sport. It seemed that as long as her body and spirit held out, she could return to the courts to reclaim her former status in the top ranks of the WTA. But would she?

Unlike Venus, Serena qualified for the WTA championships at the end of 2004. She made a strong showing early in the tournament when she defeated Myskina and Demetieva. She fell to Davenport in three sets in the third round of the round-robin tournament, but she still advanced to the finals when she defeated Amelie Mauresmo in three sets, showing in some ways the Serena of old, with aces clocked at 122 miles per hour. In the finals, she met Maria Sharapova, the 17-year-old Russian player who beat Serena at Wimbledon. Sharapova defeated Serena for a second time in the same year, winning the tournament in three sets (4–6, 6–2, 6–4) after taking six consecutive games in the final set to assure her victory. Serena suffered abdominal pain during the match, and even took a time-out during the second set for her trainer to examine her. She returned to the match, but she was in pain and had difficulty with her serve. It was a disappointing ending to her season.

Of Serena's future, Billie Jean King observed, "I think Serena is push and pull. She wants to be Miss Hollywood. She needs to decide. She could be the best ever in the history of the game" (World Tennis Network, November 2, 2004). Indeed, just a few weeks before the tennis championships, Serena was spotted at the London premiere of Pierce Brosnan and Selma Hayek's new film *After the Sunset*. Serena made a splash in her revealing red Stella McCartney dress and jewels worth $2 million, stirring controversy as photos circulated around the world. Serena spoke often of her talent in designing clothes and her enjoyment of it. She observed, "I'm an unbelievable designer. I don't know how I know and just do these things," she said. "I just start sketching and then I just know the colors and I always know the forecast. I know green and purple are going to be hot. I was born to be a designer. I worked hard to be a tennis player; I don't work hard to be a designer" (Associated Press, 2004).

No matter what their future would hold, there was no doubt that Venus and Serena made an impact on the world of sports and women's tennis. Never before have two sisters broken as many records or held as many honors in the world of women's tennis as they claimed (see appendix C and appendix D for complete lists). The women's tennis game was faster, stronger, and more competitive in response to the power and athleticism Venus and Serena brought to the sport, and they both contributed to the celebrity aura surrounding the WTA tour that brought droves of fans to the matches and to television viewing audiences. Beyond athleticism, the women's tour had an almost soap-opera effect that surrounded it, and Venus and Serena were part of the buzz. At the end of the 2004 season, commentators and observers wondered about Justine Henin-Hardenne's mysterious illness, Kim Clijster's broken engagement to Leyton Hewitt, whether Lindsay Davenport would retire, the continued force of the Russians, the up-and-coming Chinese, and, of course, what would become of the Williams sisters.

Of the two sisters, it seemed that Venus was most specific about her commitment to tennis. When Venus was asked if her career had developed in the way she anticipated, she replied, "I've reached a lot of my goals. I think when I get to the point where I have no more goals to reach, then I wouldn't have any reason to play. But I don't think I'll ever get there. And I think that I'm always expecting to get more out of myself, so obviously, I'd like to get better and stronger and more consistent. But it gives me a lot to look forward to" (ASAP Sports, Venus Williams, January 20, 2004). She further explained, "Some people want to grow up and become a star and be world-famous. Other people want to be good at what they do. And I think I'm one of those people that just I want to be good at what I do. The other stuff came second. I was just raised to be a tennis player. That's what I am" (ASAP Sports, Venus Williams, January 20, 2004).

In contrast, Serena's goals for the future seemed to be more mixed. She told reporters, "Twenty years from now, that would make me ... 32 [laughter]. I would, you know, I would see my company Aneres, we'd be really huge—hopefully. If it's blessed enough, we'd have a really solid company with my clothing line and hopefully have a few little Serenas running around—two Serenas" (ASAP Sports, Serena Williams, June 27, 2004). When asked whether she would still be involved with tennis at that time, she replied, "Oh, definitely. Hopefully by then I would have really made my mark in the movies as well, I would say about—I don't know how many films. Do a few different comedies, few different scary films or whatever. I think it would be fun. And what I made my mark in? In the movies I think I would have been successful as well, too, hopefully. I'd still only be 32, so it's kind of hard" (ASAP Sports, Serena Williams, June 27, 2004).

OFF COURT

It is difficult to predict whether Venus and Serena's impact will reach the magnitude that Muhammad Ali's did. Although Ali and the Williams sisters both seem to have their own interests at heart, Ali clearly had a more political agenda to forward around issues of black pride and his expectations of the federal government. For example, in 1968 Ali participated in the Olympic Project for Human Rights with other African American athletes, including Jim Brown, Bill Russell, and Lew Alcindor (Kareem Abdul-Jabbar), to protest the International Olympic Committee's decision to admit apartheid South Africa into the Olympic Games. The U.S. government offered no formal response, which led Ali and the other athletes to reply to this decision through the Olympic Project for Human Rights (see Entine, 2000). Although Ali's politics often included self-display (and indeed when his career and health faded, so did his political agenda), he still made an explicit effort to effect broader changes in U.S. society, particularly around questions of race (Hoberman, 1997).

Venus and Serena may choose at some point to engage a more political agenda, to tackle the challenging issues facing African Americans in U.S. society, but to date they have not, perhaps largely because of their religious beliefs. Although they both gave inspirational talks and engaged in philanthropic efforts to encourage young kids from poor urban areas to play tennis or raised money for causes like the Ronald McDonald House, their efforts were not directed toward any explicit politics or hope to change societal views or the lived experiences of African Americans in the United States. In fact, it could be argued that they perpetuated in part the misleading idea that sports would provide the way out of poverty for African American youth (see Hoberman, 1997), setting up a false dream for impressionable young people. Further, it has been argued that the ways in which they avoid discussing racism, particularly around events like Indian Wells in 2001, further perpetuates racism. The sisters refused to return to Indian Wells in 2002 and 2003, but they cast this decision around questions of entertainment rather than race. Serena explained that they did not return to the event because she and Venus liked to have fun when they played tennis, and Venus explained that her job was to entertain, and that this did not happen at Indian Wells in 2001 (Spencer, 2004).

Had they discussed openly the racism at this event, or in other tennis venues, they may have begun to shed light on this important concern. Given their celebrity, such a message would have great potential to reach a wide audience.

What the future will bring is hard to know. Venus is reportedly considering changing her name to one of African descent and going on a journey of self-discovery. Serena is considering appearing on a reality television show for Fox called *Fast Girls* (McVeigh, 2004). Whatever they do next, there is little doubt that they will do it well. Their power and influence could do much to bring about changes that extend well beyond the world of women's tennis. As Zina Garrison observed, now certainly is their time.

APPENDIXES

APPENDIX A: GRAND SLAM EVENTS

Australian Open. The tournament is held in Melbourne, Australia. Although the tournament began in 1905, women did not play until 1922. Held in January of each year, this tournament begins the Grand Slam season for professional players.

French Open. This is the second major tournament of the tennis season. The first French Open was held in 1891. It is played each year on the clay court at the Roland-Garros Stadium.

Wimbledon. Founded in 1868, the All England Lawn Tennis and Croquet Club at Wimbledon, England, has a long history and rich traditions. Players must wear white, and their trophies are presented by British royalty. Women first played singles tournaments in 1884, with Maud Watson the first champion.

U.S. Open. Played on the hard courts in Flushing Meadows, New York, the U.S. Open is known for offering the biggest prize money to its winners. The first women's singles tournament was held in 1887.

All-Williams Grand Slam Finals

2001 U.S. Open Venus defeated Serena (6–2, 6–4).

2002 French Open Serena defeated Venus (7–5, 6–3).

2002 Wimbledon Serena defeated Venus (7–6, 6–3).

2002 U.S. Open Serena defeated Venus (6–4, 6–3).

2003 Australian Open Serena defeated Venus (7–6, 3–6, 6–4).

APPENDIX B: GLOSSARY OF TERMS

backhand.   A hit in tennis in which you drive the ball across your body. If you are left-handed, you hit the ball across the right side of your body. If you are right-handed, you hit the ball across the left side of your body.

baseline.   The lines across the tennis court where the player stands to serve the ball.

court.   The rectangular area where tennis matches are played. Standard courts for singles matches measure 78 feet long and 27 feet wide. For doubles, there is four and a half feet added to the width on each side. The courts are marked with white lines for the sidelines, baselines, and service boxes. The net is midway between the two baselines.

deuce.   When both players in a tennis match have 40 points. A player needs to win the match by two points, so at least two more serves follow a deuce.

doubles.   Two players team up against another two players during a doubles match. These matches may involve two players of the same gender (women's doubles or men's doubles), or they may be mixed.

endorsement.   Money earned by professional athletes to wear products or support the advertisement of particular companies.

forehand.   Hitting the tennis ball from the side where you naturally hold your racquet. If you are right-handed, the forehand involves hitting the ball on your right side. If you are left-handed, you hit the ball on your left side.

game.   Each set comprises at least six games. A game is awarded to the player who earns the game point. Tennis scoring proceeds from love, to 15, to 30, to 40, to game point, unless there is a deuce.

> *game point.*   A point that the server or receiver needs to win the game.

Grand Slam.   Winning all four major tennis tournaments in one season (Australian Open, French Open, Wimbledon, and U.S. Open).

ground stroke.   Any shot, forehand or backhand, where the ball crosses the net and bounces.

match.   Women win a tennis match when they have won two sets out of three. To win a set, they must win at least six games. Sometimes a seventh game is required in order for the player to win by two games. Sometimes a tiebreaker is required to determine the winner of the set.

Olympic Project for Human Rights.   A group that attempted to organize black athletes in the 1960s and to link their struggle to the broader civil rights movement. The group's efforts culminated at the 1968

Olympic Games when Tommie Smith and John Carlos, two African American track athletes, raised black-gloved fists on the medal dais.

prejudice. A preconceived judgment or opinion, usually based on limited information (Tatum, 1997).

racism. A system of advantage based on race (see Tatum, 1997) that has particular histories and contexts.

rally. A play exchange between two or more players.

ranking. For the Women's Tennis Association (WTA), the player's ranking reflects her performance at major tournaments (round points) and her record against other players (quality points). The rankings are compiled over 52 weeks in a cumulative system. See the WTA website for a full listing of players' rankings (www.wtatour.com).

seeding. A graded list of players who are entering a tournament. The best players usually are seeded before the tournament begins.

serve. The serve begins each round of play in tennis. The player has to hit the ball diagonally across the court to the opponent. The player who is serving the ball has two attempts to land the ball in the opponent's court.

set. A set is a unit of scoring in tennis. The first player to win six games by a margin of at least two games has won the set. Sometimes a tie-breaker is needed.

surfaces. Tennis courts have one of three different surfaces: clay, grass, or hard court.

> *clay.* Tennis courts made of crushed stone, brick, or shale. This is a soft court surface that gives way under the player's feet, and it is considered to be a slow surface for tennis. The French Open is played on a clay court.

> *grass.* This surface, with very short and well-maintained grass, is similar to the putting greens found on golf courses. It is difficult to maintain and suited to only certain players' styles (such as those with big serves). Some are wondering if this surface will become obsolete.

> *hard court.* These courts are made of asphalt or concrete and then painted with acrylic paint that is mixed with sand to give it texture. This court is considered to be a fast surface, and it is the most common court in the United States. Both the U.S. Open and the Australian Open are played on hard courts.

umpire. The official who controls the player, the game, and the line judges. A match referee can be called from the stands to settle a controversial call.

volley. Playing the tennis ball in the air before it bounces.

Women's Tennis Association (WTA). This is the governing body for women's professional tennis (see www.wtatour.com).

APPENDIX C: VENUS WILLIAMS'S RECORDS AND AWARDS (ADAPTED FROM VENUS WILLIAMS OFFICIAL WEB SITE)

Records

Fastest serve: In 1998, Venus's serve was clocked at 127 miles per hour, a women's world record.

Most lucrative endorsement deal for a woman in sport: Reebok contract for $40 million.

Sports Illustrated Athlete of the Year (2000).

Awards

- As part of Family Circle Cup Community Outreach program, the tournament donated $20,000 in Venus's name to the Charleston County School of the Arts, the Minority Business Development program, and Dress-for-Success.
- Ranked number 4 on 2003 Top 10 Most-Marketable Female Athletes, as published by *Sports Business Daily* (determined by a poll of 60 marketers, sponsorship consultants, and members of the media); (1) Serena Williams, (2) Annika Sorenstam (golf), (3) Mia Hamm (soccer), (5) Lisa Leslie (basketball).
- Along with her mother and her sister Serena, Venus was the featured cover story for the May 2003 issue of *Ebony* magazine.
- In 2003, at the 34th NAACP Image Awards, Venus received the President's Award with her sister Serena.
- Venus and Serena Williams were first duo to reach four consecutive Grand Slam finals in the Open era.
- Venus was reelected to the WTA Tour Players' Council in 2002.
- On February 25, 2002, Venus became the 10th world number 1 player in the history of WTA rankings and the first African American (male or female), overtaking compatriot Jennifer Capriati and becoming the fourth different player ranked number 1 in four months (with Hingis, Davenport, and Capriati).

- Venus's endorsement contract with Reebok is the largest ever awarded to a woman athlete.
- Personal fashion line: Venus Collection by Wilson's Leather.
- Venus and Serena are the first sisters in tennis history each to have won a Grand Slam singles title; the first sisters to meet in a WTA Tour final (1999 Miami, won by Venus); the first sisters to win Olympic gold medal in doubles (2000); the only sisters in the twentieth century to win a Grand Slam doubles title together (they won three).
- Venus won the 2002 ESPY Award for Best Female Athlete and Best Female Tennis Player for her play in 2001.
- Venus was ranked number 25 on the *Ladies' Home Journal* 30 Most Powerful Women in America List released in November 2001.
- Venus was voted the 2001 WTA Tour Player of the Month for March, July, August, and September; 2000 WTA Tour Player of the Year and Doubles Team of the Year with sister Serena; *Sports Illustrated for Women* Sportswoman of the Year.
- One of five female tennis players named to the *Forbes* magazine Power 100 in Fame and Fortune list at number 62 (no other female athletes made the list).
- 1998 *Tennis* magazine's Most Improved Player.
- Recipient of the 1997 WTA Tour Most Impressive Newcomer Award (won by her sister Serena a year later).
- Named U.S. Olympic Committee Female Athlete of the Month for September 1997, becoming only the third tennis player to win the award.
- 1997 *Tennis* magazine's Most Improved Female Pro.
- Received an award in 1995 from the Sports Image Foundation for conducting tennis clinics in low-income areas.
- By age 12, accumulated a 63–0 record in USTA sectional play in southern California.

Tennis Wins

2003 Australian Open (singles) finalist.
2003 Australian Open (doubles) champion.
2003 Wimbledon (singles) finalist.
2002 U.S. Open (singles) finalist.
2002 Wimbledon (singles) finalist.
2002 Wimbledon (doubles) champion.

2002 French Open (singles) finalist.

2002 Bausch and Lomb (singles) champion.

2002 Proximus Diamond Games (singles) champion.

2002 Gaz de France (singles) champion.

2002 Thalgo Australian Women's Hardcourts (singles) champion.

2001 U.S. Open (singles) champion.

2001 Wimbledon (singles) champion.

2001 Ericsson Open (singles) champion.

2001 Australian Open (doubles) champion.

2000 Wimbledon (singles and doubles) champion.

2000 U.S. Open (singles) champion.

2000 Olympics (singles and doubles) champion.

1999 French Open (doubles) champion.

1999 U.S. Open (doubles) champion.

1999 Oklahoma City (singles) champion.

1999 Miami (singles) champion.

1999 Hamburg (singles) champion.

1999 Italian Open (singles) champion.

1999 New Haven (singles) champion.

1999 Zurich (singles) champion.

1998 Oklahoma City (singles and doubles) champion.

1998 Miami (singles) champion.

1998 Grand Slam Cup (singles) champion.

1997 U.S. Open (singles) finalist.

APPENDIX D: SERENA WILLIAMS'S RECORDS AND AWARDS (ADAPTED IN PART FROM SERENA WILLIAMS'S OFFICIAL WEB SITE)

- Won the 2004 ESPY Award for best female athlete for the second year.
- Serena Slam: With her win in the Australian Open in 2003, Serena won all four Grand Slam tennis tournaments in a row. She did achieve a Grand Slam by winning them all in the same season.
- Serena was the second African American woman to win a Grand Slam tournament in U.S. history when she won the U.S. Open in 1999. Althea Gibson was the only other African American woman to do so, winning her titles in the 1950s.

- Named 2004 Family Circle/Prudential Financial Player Who Makes a Difference Award, given annually to a female professional tennis player who has made outstanding contributions of both time and energy to worthy causes.
- Along with Henin-Hardenne, nominated for Laureus World Sportswoman of the Year Award, presented in May 2004 for outstanding achievements in sport during the previous 12 months.
- In an on-court ceremony just before the Amelia Island opening match (April 7, 2004), Shock Absorber presented the 2003 Women's Wimbledon Champion with $66,800, equalizing the men's prize money.
- Featured in the 2004 40th anniversary edition of the *Sports Illustrated* swimsuit issue.
- Feature story on ESPN one-hour special, "All Exclusive with Ahmad" (broadcast on February 13, 2004).
- Named by *Sports Illustrated* as the third most influential minority in sports (behind Robert Johnson and Tiger Woods).
- Ad for the Breast Cancer Awareness Campaign is featured in the October 2003 issues of *Vogue, Essence, Lucky,* and *Self.*
- Among the few high-profile celebrities who designed a shoe for a Stuart Weisman charity auction.
- Ranked number 1 on the 2003 Top 10 Most-Marketable Female Athletes, as published by *Sports Business Daily* (determined by a poll of 60 marketers, sponsorship consultants, and members of the media); (2) Annika Sorenstam (golf), (3) Mia Hamm (soccer), (4) Venus Williams (tennis), (5) Lisa Leslie (basketball).
- Honored as the 2003 Laureus World Sportswoman of the Year (award statuette presented by sister Venus Williams).
- Received the 2003 Celebrity Role Model Award from Avon Foundation for her charitable work in breast cancer awareness.
- Honored by the WTA Tour with a stadium-court trophy presentation at Charleston, South Carolina, for becoming the fifth player in tennis history to complete a non-calendar-year Grand Slam (following her triumph over sister Venus at the 2003 Australian Open), nicknamed the Serena Slam.
- Named the WTA Tour Player of the Month for July 2003 by the International Tennis Writers Association.
- Voted by the International Tennis Writers Association as Player of the Month for January 2003 and March 2003, her sixth and seventh times selected for the monthly award since the program's

inception in January 2001 (received the honor five times in 2002, more than any other player).

- Appeared in the *Sports Illustrated* 2003 swimsuit issue.
- Cover stories in *Parade* (March 16, 2003), *ESPN Magazine* (March 31, 2003), *Sports Illustrated* (May 26, 2003), and, along with her mother and her sister Venus, *Ebony* (May 2003); in a *Vogue* photo spread (April 2003).
- In 2003, at the 34th NAACP Image Awards, received the President's Award with her sister Venus.
- 2003 recipient of the Big Brothers Big Sisters of Greater Los Angeles and the Inland Empire's Young Heroes Award and the ESPY Female Athlete of the Year and Female Tennis Player of the Year.
- Featured in December 2003 issue of *InStyle* as a "shining star."
- Won four straight Grand Slam tournament singles titles (2002 French Open, 2002 Wimbledon, 2002 U.S. Open, 2003 Australian Open) becoming the fifth woman to hold all four titles at once (Maureen Connolly, Margaret Smith Court, Martina Navratilova, Steffi Graf) and the ninth to win each in a career.
- Along with sister Venus, they were the first duo to reach four straight Grand Slam finals in the Open era.
- Serena Williams and sister Venus Williams are the first sisters in tennis history each to have won a Grand Slam singles title and the first sisters to meet in a WTA Tour final (1999 Miami, won by Venus).
- First sisters to win Olympic gold medal in doubles (2000).
- Only sisters in the 20th century to win a Grand Slam doubles title together (won three).
- 2002 honors included being ranked number 7 among A&E Cable Network and *Biography* magazine's 10 most significant people contending for the 2002 biography of the year; named by *People* magazine as one of the 25 Most Intriguing People in 2002; named by *Ebony* magazine as one of the 57 Most Intriguing African Americans in 2002; named one of the BBC's 2002 Sports Personalities of the Year; recognized by *Time* magazine as one of the People Who Mattered in 2002; voted best female athlete in the world for 2002 by the Associated Press and by the Spanish news agency EFE; named 2002 WTA Tour Player of the Year; named 2002 ITF Women's Singles World Champion; appeared on the cover of *Tennis* (May 2002, with Venus), *Jet* (July 22, 2002), *ESPN* (August 19, 2002), *Ebony* (October 2002), *Savoy* (November 2002), *New*

York Post (August 26, 2002), *USA Today* (November 1, 2002), *Sports Illustrated for Kids* (November/December 2002), and *Biography* (January 2003).

- Selected as one of the 12 Coolest Girls in Sports in the November 2001 issue of *Sports Illustrated Women*.
- In 2000, one of five female tennis players named to the *Forbes* Power 100 in Fame and Fortune list at number 68 (no other female athletes made the list); along with sister Venus received the 2000 Achievement Award at the Teen Awards; 2000 WTA Tour Doubles Team of the Year with sister Venus.
- In 1999, named the *Tennis* magazine Player of the Year and the WTA Tour Most Improved Player; named the United States Olympic Committee's Female Athlete of the Month for September 1999 (along with male winner Andre Agassi), marking the first time tennis players swept the monthly awards; named one of *People* magazine's 25 Most Intriguing People of 1999.
- Recipient of the 1998 WTA Tour Most Impressive Newcomer Award, which was won by her sister Venus in 1997; named 1998 *Tennis* magazine/Rolex Rookie of the Year.
- Donated $10,000 to Clarendon (South Carolina) School District 1, where tennis legend Althea Gibson was born: $8,000 for computer laptops and $2,000 for the Serena Williams Scholarship.
- WTA Tour mentor was Zina Garrison in the Partners for Success Alumni program.

Recognition as Sisters

In 1999, the sisters made history as they each won singles titles in a professional tournament within a week of each other. Venus won in Oklahoma, and Serena won the Paris Indoors.

1999 French Open Doubles (first sisters to win a doubles title in the twentieth century).

Received the 2000 Achievement Award at the Teen Awards, the Women's Sports Foundation's Athlete of the Year Award, and a Laureus Sports Award.

On July 8, 2002, Serena achieved the number 1 ranking with the WTA, the first time two sisters had both earned this status.

When Venus won Wimbledon in 2000, it marked the first time two sisters both had won a Grand Slam tournament (Serena won the U.S. Open in 1999).

First sisters to win U.S. Olympic gold medals for their doubles victory at the Olympics in Sydney, Australia (2000).

Tennis Wins

2005 Australian Open champion
2004 French Open quarter finalist
2004 Wimbledon finalist
2004 U.S. Open quarter finalist
2004 Miami champion
2004 Beijing champion
2003 Australian champion
2003 French semifinalist
2003 Wimbledon champion
2003 Paris (indoor) champion
2003 Miami champion
2002 French champion
2002 Wimbledon champion
2002 U.S. Open champion
2002 Miami champion
2002 Scottsdale champion
2002 Rome champion
2002 Tokyo champion
2002 Leipzig champion
2001 Australian quarter finalist
2001 French quarter finalist
2001 Wimbledon quarter finalist
2001 U.S. Open quarter finalist
2001 Canadian Open champion
2001 Season Ending champion
2001 Indian Wells champion
2000 Wimbledon semifinalist
2000 U.S. Open finalist
2000 Hannover champion
2000 Los Angeles champion
2000 Tokyo champion
1999 U.S. Open champion
1999 Paris (indoor) champion
1999 Indian Wells champion
1999 Los Angeles champion

APPENDIX E: A NOTE ON SOURCES

A variety of resources have been used in writing this book, including personal correspondence with Carlos Fleming, a representative of the Williams sisters. Attempts were made to correspond directly with Venus and Serena, but to no avail. Fleming explained to me that any biography written at this point in their lives would necessarily be devoid of some major accomplishments the sisters would achieve because Venus and Serena were still quite early in their careers (personal communication, December 15, 2003). Although this is certainly true, it does seem that there is much to observe and understand from Venus and Serena's lives, even while they are young.

We live in an information age that provides many valuable and reliable sources of information that are useful in putting together the story of Venus and Serena's lives. The DVD *Raising Tennis Aces: The Williams Story* contains extensive interviews with Richard, Venus, and Serena, and there are countless transcripts from news conferences, television talk shows, magazine interviews, and other sources that allow us to understand much of their lives in their own words. All dialogue in this book is directly quoted from sources such as these. None of the dialogue has been created.

Much of the quoted material throughout this book is cited from the ASAP Sports Web site (http://www.asapsports.com), which contains transcripts of interviews conducted immediately after a tennis match. Direct quotes from this Web site and can be found by searching the tennis interviews by date. Any direct quotes that are supported with a Harpo, 2002, date are from Venus and Serena's appearance on *The Oprah Winfrey Show* with their mother, Oracene Price, and their sisters, Yetunde, Lyndrea, and Isha. Other direct quotes are cited by source.

In addition, some key Web sites were helpful in the research for this book. Reports of typical days and not-so-typical days in chapter 3 are based on information from Venus Williams's official Web site (http://www.venuswilliams.com). Much of the information in chapter 4 is drawn from Serena's official Web site (http://www.serenawilliams.com), particularly the information on her favorite shopping places and favorite restaurants. These Web sites, designed and maintained by TWI Interactive, were launched with much fanfare by the girls on October 30, 2003. Both Web sites contain up-to-date information on their tennis and other aspects of their lives.

A full list of resources used in researching this book is available at the end of the book.

REFERENCES

Aronson, V. (2001). *Women who win: Venus and Serena Williams*. Philadelphia: Chelsea House.

ASAP Sports. (n.d.). Serena Williams. Retrieved from http://www.asapsports. com/tennis/000UZ/WilliamsSerena.html

ASAP Sports. (n.d.). Venus Williams. Retrieved from http://www.asapsports. com/tennis/000UZ/WilliamsVenus.html

Associated Press. (2004, November 16). Serena Williams says she's an ace at clothing design. *London Free Press*. Retrieved November 16, 2004, from http:// www.canoe.ca/NewsStand/LondonFreePress/Today/2004/11/16/716231. html

Austin, T. (2004, September 7). Without Henin-Hardenne, tournament is wide open: Stunning loss by no. 1 seed shows how deep women's tennis has become. Retrieved September 15, 2004, from http://msnbc.msn.com/ id/5927033

Badenhausen, K. (2004, June 28). Best paid athletes: Uneven playing field. *Forbes*, Retrieved November 3, 2004, from http://www.forbes.com/ lists/2004/06/28/cz_kb_0628gender.html

Barra, A. (2003, October 2). Rush Limbaugh was right: Donovan McNabb isn't a great quarterback, and the media do overrate him because he is black. Retrieved April 17, 2005, from http://www.slate.msn.com/id/2089193

Bateson, M.C. (1989). *Composing a life*. New York: Grove Press.

Berman, M. (2004, September 11). Dad: Umpire Prejudiced. Retrieved April 18, 2005, from http://www.blackathletesportsnetwork.net/artman/publish/ article_0332.shtml

Black Athlete Sports Network. (2003, July 7). Racism abounds at Wimbledon. Retrieved October 17, 2004, from http://www.blackathlete.com/Tennis/tennis070703.html

Bohnert, C. (2004, August 11). TENNIS: USTA Statement on Serena Williams withdraw from 2004 Olympic Games. Retrieved April 7, 2005, from http://www.USOlympicteam.com/73_23345.htm

Chappell, K. (2002, October). Serena as you've never seen her before: Talks about her femininity, her love life, her father. *Ebony*, 164.

Clarey, C. (2004, July 4). Sharapova conquers Wimbledon. *New York Times*, section 8 p. 1.

Clarke, R. (2003, September 15). Sister was "rock" behind Williams success. Retrieved March 31, 2005, from http://news.bbc.co.uk/1/hi/world/americas/3110564.stm

Cortez, A. (2000, September 26). Look who's got a bad attitude. *Denver Post*, p. B07.

Crockett, S. (2002, August 3). Serena Williams stalker arrested again. Retrieved April 14, 2004, from http://www.bet.com

Ebony. (2003). Mother power: Serena and Venus Williams on the fabulous Oracene, mother of the Williams dynasty. *Ebony*, 156.

Entine, J. (2000). *Taboo: Why black athletes dominate sports and why we're afraid to talk about it.* New York: Public Affairs.

Evans, R. (2003, March 30). Williams keen to serve Brits. *Sunday Times*, p. 18.

Fendrich, H. (2004, July 4). Sharapova stuns Williams to win Wimbledon. *Centre Daily Times*, p. B12.

Flatman, B. (2003, January 26). Sisters steer clear of battle of the sexes. *Sunday Times*, p. 23.

Frammolino, R. (2003, January 29). Serena Williams: Tennis. Retrieved August 31, 2004, from http://www.authorsden.com/visit/viewnews.asp?AuthorID=7185&id=5034

Garber, G. (2002, July 22). Stalking threat modern-day reality. Retrieved July 26, 2004, from http://espn.go.com/tennis/usopen02/s/2002/0905/1427462.html

Gordon, M. (2004, July 4). Russian crowned queen of SW19. *Scotsman*, p. 9.

Guardian. (2004, January 15). Williams sisters a double-act to follow. Retrieved April 1, 2005, from http://www.theage.com.au/articles/004/01/14/1073877899135.html?oneclick=true

Hall, S. (1997). Race, culture, and communication: Looking backward and forward at cultural studies. In John Storey (Ed.), *What is cultural studies? A reader* (pp. 336–343). New York: Arnold.

Harpo Productions, Inc. (2002, November 27). *The Oprah Winfrey Show*, "Venus and Serena Williams." Livingston, NJ: Burrell's Information Services.

Hauser, T. (1991). *Muhammad Ali: His life and times*. New York: Simon & Schuster.

Hayes, A. (2002, July 7). "Offensive, ridiculous and unfair"—Oracene Williams mounts strong defense of her daughters. Retrieved April 8, 2005, from http://sport.independent.co.uk/tennis/story.jsp?story=312739

Hernnstein, R., & Murray, C. (1996). *The bell curve: Intelligence and class structure in American life*. New York: Free Press.

Heywood, L., & Dworkin, S. (2003). *Built to win: The female athlete as cultural icon*. Minneapolis: University of Minnesota Press.

Hoberman, J. (1997). *Darwin's athletes: How sport has damaged black America and preserved the myth of race*. New York: Mariner Books.

Hruby, P. (2000, May 22). Tennis racket. Retrieved September 19, 2004, from http://www.findarticles.com/p/articles/mi_m1571/is_19_16/ai_62349861/print

Hubbard, L. (2002, June 18). Richard Williams, role model. *The Progressive Media Project*. Retrieved July 22, 2004, from http://www.progressive.org/Media%20Project%202/mphj1802.html

International Herald Tribune. (2003, January). For Williams sisters, are racism and sexism in the crowd? Retrieved October 16, 2004, from http://www.icare.to/archivejanuary2003.html

Ithaca Times. (2004, June 17). Courting trouble: Tempestuous love lives, a sister murdered in a gang land shooting, and now a vicious custody battled with her ex-jailbird lover. Retrieved July 21, 2004, from http://www.zwire.com/site/news.cfm?newsid=11998566&BRD=1395&PAG=740&dept_id=226957&rfi=6

Jacques, M. (2003, June 25). Tennis is racist: It's time we did something about it. *Guardian*. Retrieved April 7, 2005, from http://sport.guardian.co.uk/wimbledon2003/story/1,,984568,00.html

Jenkins, S. (2001, February 1). Netcetera: My point: Royalties for Venus and Serena. *Tennis.*Retrieved April 8, 2005, from http://tennis.com.

Jervis, D. (2002). *Raising tennis aces: The Williams story*. Santa Monica, CA: Xenon Entertainment.

Jet. (2001, April 9). Richard Williams laments his tennis star daughters are subjected to racial slurs, denies rigging their matches. *Jet*, 51.

Jet. (2001, July 9). Fired white sportscaster apologizes for remarks about Venus and Serena Williams, gets rehired. *Jet*, 32.

Lusetich, R. (2004, June 26). Venus wanes in grand decision. *Weekend Australian*, p. 52.

Malveaux, J. (2000). Affirmative action advertising? No way. Retrieved October 21, 2004, from http://www.juliannemalveaux.com/affirm_action_adv.htm

McVeigh, K. (2004, August 14). Williams Sisters: Is anyone for tennis? Retrieved November 4, 2004, from http://thescotsman.scotsman.com/index.cfm?id=937352004

Michie, R. (2003, June). The world according to Oracene Price. *Tennis.* Retrieved July 21, 2004, from http://tennis.com

Olson, L. (2002, September 8). They're champions off court as sisters, too. *New York Daily News*, p. 44.

Puma, M. (2001, September 8). Venus defeats Serena in 2001 U.S. Open final. *ESPN Classic.* Retrieved July 21, 2004, from http://espn.go.com/classic/s/add_williams_venus_and_serena.html

Riley, R. (1997). Introduction to Title IX: 25 years of progress. Retrieved July 13, 2004, from http://www.ed.gov/pubs/TitleIX/part1.html

Rineberg, D. (2003). *Venus and Serena Williams: My seven years as hitting coach for the Williams sisters.* Hollywood, FL: Frederick Fell Publishers.

Robbins, C.G. (2004). Racism and the authority of neoliberalism: A review of three new books on the persistence of racial inequality in a color-blind era. *Journal for Critical Education Policy Studies, 2*(2). Retrieved October 15, 2004, from http://www.jceps.com/index.php?pageID=article&articleID=35

Robertson, D. (2004, September 8). Serena cries foul in quarter loss; Capriati reaches semis after several calls go her way. *Houston Chronicle*, p. 3.

Rovell, D. (2003, July 24). Puma back in Serena endorsement derby. ESPN Sports Business. Retrieved November 3, 2004, from http://espn.go.com/sportsbusiness/s/2003/0724/1585126.html

Samuels, A. (2001, July 2). Life with father. *Newsweek*, 46.

Schiffman, B. (2002). Serena heads west. http://www.forbes.com/2002/12/06/cx_bs_1206movers.html

Sparling, K. (2000). *Serena and Venus Williams.* New York: Warwick Press.

Spencer, N. (2004). Sister act VI: Venus and Serena Williams at Indian Wells: "Sincere fictions and white racism." *Journal of Sport and Social Issues, 28*(2), 115–135.

Tatum, B. (1997). *Why are all the black kids sitting together in the cafeteria? And other conversations about race.* New York: Basic Books.

Toombs, E. (2003, July 18). Goodbye Toronto, hello Hollywood! Retrieved April 1, 2001, from http://www.tennis-ontheline.com/aw/aw030728.htm

Tresniowski, A., and Rozsa, L. (2004, June 28). On the move. *People*, 138–139.

Vecsey, G. (2002, February). Racism and tennis. Retrieved April 14, 2004, from http://tennis.com

Watkins, S.C. (1999). *Representing: Hiphop culture and the production of black cinema.* Chicago: University of Chicago Press.

Watterson, J. (2003, June 6). "Serena Slam" ends in tears. *Irish Times*, p. 21.

Wertheim, L. J. (2002). *Venus envy: Power games, teenage vixens, and million-dollar egos on the women's tennis tour.* New York: Perennial.

Wertheim, L. J. (2004, September 6). Minority rule? Move over, Venus and Serena. *Sports Illustrated,* p. 16.

Wilstein, S. (2000, July 8). Williams captures Wimbledon. Retrieved December 23, 2004, from www.ottawalynx.com/SlamTennisWimbledon00/jul8_will.html

World Tennis Network. (2004, July 4). Williams family reign ends at Wimbledon. Retrieved from www.serena.wtnworld.com/serena/News/2366

World Tennis Network. (2004, November 2). Venus goes looking for form. Retrieved November 13, 2004, from http://venus.wtnworld.com/venus/News/3244

WEB SITES OF INTEREST

Jehovah's Witnesses. http://www.watchtower.org

Serena Williams Official Web Site. http://www.serenawilliams.com

Venus and Serena Williams Tutorial/Tennis Academy. http://www.venusserenatennisacademy.org

Venus Williams Official Web Site. http://www.venuswilliams.com

Women's Tennis Association. http://www.wtatour.com

INDEX

Ali, Muhammad, 87–88, 91
American Express, 80, 82
Aneres, 84, 90
Angelou, Maya, 37
Austin, Tracy, 24, 49, 65
Australian Open, 36, 43, 54, 60
Avon, 68, 80

Baker, Dusty, 67
Bandenhausen, Kurt, 82
Basketball, 40
Battle of the Sexes, 72
Becker, Boris, 46
Black youth culture in the United
   States, 70
Braasch, Karsten, 72
Brandy, 37–38, 40, 53, 80, 84
Brooks, Kerrie, 49

Capriati, Jennifer, 24, 32, 35, 51, 79
Carillo, Mary, 68
Celebrity, 31, 73, 77–80; crossover
   pop-culture star, 79–80; drawbacks
   to, 78–80
Clijster, Kim, 90

Clinton, Bill, 57–58
Commission on Opportunity in Ath-
   letics, 5
Compton, California, 16, 21–23,
   29–30, 44, 46, 57, 64, 80
Confederate flag boycott by NAACP,
   19
Connolly, Maureen, 36
Connor, Jimmy, 72
Court, Margaret, 36, 76

Davenport, Lindsay, 1, 28, 49, 73,
   89, 90
Demetieva, Elena, 89
Dogs, 26, 39
Dokic, Jelena, 51
Dolls, 46, 69–70
Doublemint gum, 68, 81

Easy-E, 44
Education, 25, Art Institute, 25;
   Driftwood Academy, 25, 37; im-
   portance of, 11, 24, 45, 77; Palm
   Beach Community College, 25
Endorsements, 68–69, 71, 80–82

Entine, John, 66–67
ESPY Awards, 16, 37
Evert, Chris Lloyd, 1, 36, 52, 68, 71

Fame, problems of, 46. *See also* Celebrity
Fashion, 34, 82–84, 89
Films: depicting ghetto, 16; Serena's favorites, 37; Serena's roles in, 38
French Open, 3, 26, 36, 41, 49, 60, 65, 78

Garrison, Zina, 1–3, 32, 53–54, 92; Zina Garrison All Court Tennis Academy, 3
Gender, 4–6, 63, 71, 73; pay inequities in professional tennis, 4, 72–73. *See also* Women in sport
Ghetto Cinderellas, 22
Gibson, Althea, 1–3, 5
Gimblestob, Justin, 60
Graf, Steffi, 24, 36, 46, 48, 51, 52, 54

Hair beads, 35, 67–68
Haynes, Angela, 76
Henin-Hardenne, Justine, 65, 90
Hewitt, Leyton, 90
Hingis, Martina, 36, 51, 53, 59, 61, 63, 68, 69, 73, 79
How to Play Tennis: Learn How to Play Tennis the Williams Sisters' Way, 26

Imus, Don, 71
Indian Wells, 65–66, 91

Jacques, Martin, 65
Jehovah's Witnesses, 19–20
Jenkins, Sally, 73
Jenkins, Scoville, 75, 76
Jones, Marion, 6, 81, 84

King, Billy Jean, 4, 72, 88, 89
Kournikova, Anna, 6, 53, 73

Lactose intolerance, 81
Limbaugh, Rush, 69

Macci, Rick, 35, 46–48
Maleeva, Manuaela and Katarina, 43
Malveaux, Julianne, 69
Mauresmo, Amelie, 89
McDonald's, 68, 80, 83
McEnroe, John, 28, 44–45, 46, 53, 71, 72
McEnroe, Patrick, 72
McNabb, Donovan, 69
McNeil, Lori, 54
Minter, Ann and Elizabeth, 43
Mirnyi, Max, 60
Modeling, 68
Molitar, Melanie, 51
Myskina, Anastasia, 89

Navratilova, Martina, 48, 52, 59, 65, 69, 71, 74
Nike, 80, 82

Olympic Project for Human Rights, 91
OWL Foundation, 15, 38

Parche, Guenter, 79
Pierce, Mary, 35, 51
Prejudice, 63, 64
Price, Isha, 12, 18, 22
Price, Lyndrea, 12, 18, 34, 84
Price, Yetunde, 12, 15–19, 70
Puma, 68, 80

Race, 9, 63, 69; racial barriers for African American women in sport, 3, 71; racism, 9, 13, 36, 49, 63–67,

69, 71, 74, 87–88, 91–92; racism on WTA tour, 53–54

Ratner, Brett, 41

Raymond, Lisa, 54

Reading, 23, 37; American Library Association's Celebrity READ campaign, 38

Reebok, 68, 80, 82, and Diane von Furstenberg, 83

Reece, Gabriel, 6

Riggs, Bobby, 72

Rineburg, David, 13, 48

Robinson, Jackie, 74

Rosenburg, Sid, 71

Rubin, Chandra, 28, 54, 59

Ruzici, Virginia, 12

Sabatini, Gabriella, 46, 52

Sampras, Pete, 46, 54

Sanchez-Vicario, Arantxa, 29, 48

Schumaker, Michael, 82

Schwartz, Alan, 75

Seles, Monica, 36, 46, 59, 72, 79

Selling black bodies, 67–69

Serena Slam, 36–37

Sharapova, Maria, 2, 6, 89

Sisterhood, 15,18, 21; sisters in tennis, 43

Snoop Doggy Dogg, 44

Snyder, Jimmy "the Greek," 66, 67

Social class issues, 10–11, 16, 18, 22, 63, 70, 91

Spirlea, Irina, 65

Sports Illustrated, 5, 75, 80

Sprem, Karolina, 3

Stevenson, Alexandra, 28, 54, 59

Stromeyer, Albrecht, 78–79

Stubbs, Rennae, 54, 59

Tang, Li, 60

Tennis: history of, 4; parents' role in, 51–52; parents as coach, 51–52; professional earnings, 4; Williams' training schedule, 48. See also Williams, Serena; Williams, Venus

Tennis Monthly Recap, 54

Tian Tian, Sun, 60

Title IX of the Education Act of 1972, 4–5

Travel: abroad, 26, 65; in the U.S., 26

Trump, Donald, 72

Ubergirl, 6

Unilever Close-up Toothpaste, 81

U.S. invasion of Iraq, 65

U.S. Olympics, 24, 28, 29, 31, 32, 58, 59, 60, 83, 84

U.S. Open, 9, 21–22, 31–33, 35, 36, 43, 44, 50, 53, 56–57, 59, 63, 65, 69, 74, 75, 80, 83

U.S.T.A. junior circuit, 45–47, 50, 53, 68

Venus and Serena Williams Tutorial/ Tennis Academy, 38

V Starr Interiors, 26, 84

Watkins, S. Craig, 70

Watson, Maud and Lillian, 43

Wertheim, L. Jon, 50, 53–54, 75

Williams, Oracene Price, 1, 12, 14, 19, 22–23, 44, 47, 49, 51, 65, 67–68, 70, 71, 87, 88; athleticism, 12; attitudes toward women, 73, 74; as coach, 51–52; custody of Yetunde's children, 17–18; disposition, 15; divorce from Richard, 15, 50; importance of self-esteem, 13; marriage to Richard, 12; as mother, 15; and religion, 19

Williams, Richard, 22–24, 45, 46, 47, 48, 49, 51, 60, 63, 65, 67, 73, 77, 80, 87, 88; behavior at tennis tournaments, 43, 50, 55–56; business ventures, 12; childhood, 10–11, 37; as coach, 10, 44, 48, 50, 52; disposition, 13; divorce from Oracene, 15; as a father, 10–11, 13–14; first family, 11, 14, 70; planning, 12–13; storytelling, 11; views on interracial marriage, 41

Williams, Serena: acting, 38–39; antipathy toward, 53; athletic build, 35; boyfriends, 40; clothing, 32; competing with Venus, 43, 54–58; disposition of, 33, 54, 56; doubles, 58–60; favorite places to shop, 37; film roles, 38; future, 89, 90; future in film, 90–91; hobbies, 33, 37; homes, 39–40; injuries, 31, 36, 89; on looking good, 34, 83; pet dogs, 39; philanthropy, 38; practice/training schedule, 45, 48–49; retirement, 88; as role model, 75, 84–85; shopping, 37, 39; as sister, 33–35, 54; style, 32, 34 -35; as superstar, 31–32; television roles and appearances, 31, 38, 79; tennis, 35; turning professional, 36; and Venus, 33; Wilson Leather Products, 68, 80, 83

Williams, Venus: antipathy toward, 53; boyfriend, 29; competing with Serena, 43, 54–58; disposition of, 22–23, 28–29, 33, 43, 54–55, 56; doubles, 58–60; favorite music, 26; future, 89, 90; hobbies, 23, 26; guitar, 25–26; high school, 24–25; junior circuit, 45–46; language study, 26; other sports, 26–27; pay equity in women's tennis, 72; pet dogs, 26; practice/training schedule, 25, 45, 48–49; retirement from tennis, 28, 88; as role model for young people, 75, 84; serve speed, 45–46; as sister, 21–22, 29; as sports fan, 28; television appearances, 79; turning professional 24; typical days, 25–27

Wilson tennis racquets, 80

Wimbledon, 1–2, 6, 9, 21, 26, 29, 36, 43, 44, 52, 57, 59, 60, 63, 72, 75, 77, 78, 80, 83, 89

Winfrey, Oprah, 15, 26, 33, 34, 77; *Oprah Winfrey Show*, 1, 15, 18, 79, 83

Women in sport, 6, 71

Women's Tennis Association (WTA), 2, 9, 20, 24, 33, 36, 44, 54, 65, 88, 89; challenges of, 53; charismatic nature of, 52, 73, 90; international nature of, 54; pay equity, 72–73; racism and, 53–54

Woods, Tiger, 69, 70–71, 82

Young, Donald, 76

About the Author

JACQUELINE EDMONDSON is Assistant Professor of Education at Penn State University. She teaches undergraduate and graduate courses in language and literacy education, and she researches and writes about education policy.